Call to Dooty

A gentleman's guide to the harrowing adventure of fatherhood

By DANIEL TRAFFORD

CALL TO DOOTY

A gentleman's guide to the harrowing adventure of fatherhood

Copyright © 2014 by Daniel Trafford
Illustrations by Daniel Trafford
Cover design by Mary A. Trafford

ISBN-13: 978-1495325779
ISBN-10: 1495325776

For my children, without whom,
this book would not be possible

CONTENTS

1. INTRODUCTION

When you become a father, there's an awful lot you're not prepared for.

I don't mean crying babies, sleepless nights, strains on your marriage. You'll be warned about all those things by dozens of people before your baby draws its first breath. And you can never really be prepared for them anyway.

No, I'm talking about the things they don't tell you about in the Lamaze classes or the parenting books. So I decided to write this one just for new fathers, thinking that maybe they'll have a better shot at knowing what they'll be dealing with. After all, before you start out on a journey, it's a good idea to know where you're going.

Don't get me wrong. This isn't one of those books that presents fathers as fish out of water, like those sitcoms that show dads alone with their children doing stupid things like putting duct tape on a diaper because, shucks and golly, they're just too dumb to figure out how it works.

Believe me, fatherhood is humorous enough without having to resort to these kinds of clichés for a cheap laugh.

I have great kids. My 16-year-old daughter loves to go on and on about what book she's reading, or what TV show she's watching — and I get an endless stream of scuttlebutt about the intrigues in her circle of friends. My 6-year-old son is more comfortable having an insightful conversation about the meaning of existence over his morning bowl of cornflakes. I love each and every minute I spend with them.

Wasn't always that way, though.

There was a time when they would scream and scream. They couldn't eat, poop or get dressed without my constant attention. And don't even get me started on their social skills.

That period of time was called infancy. I loved them then as I love them now. I just like them a lot better now that they can eat, get dressed and go to the bathroom all by themselves.

I suspect that there are other fathers out there like me — those who are hesitant to admit that infancy is anything but a constant bleeping joy. I understand and I don't blame them.

So, for all those fathers, I wanted to write this book. I don't want to shock you; I don't want to scare you off. And I certainly don't want to make light of fatherhood. Because of circumstances and choice, I have spent a lot of time with my infant children.

But it's getting through infancy and toddlerhood that makes being a father that much more rewarding. Today more than ever, the role of the father is needed in helping children grow into good, honest, decent adults — those that say please and thank you and know how to use their freakin' turn signals.

I suspect that many fathers get scared by infants and tend to shy away rather than barrel in boldly, fight the good fight, and change diapers like a man.

But all of this is extremely rewarding. And I don't mean that the way women do — with a warm maternal feeling; for indeed, you'll hate every minute of it. No, what I mean is that you'll be rewarded with a human being who can think, talk, wipe itself and has its own little personality.

Remember, infancy is nothing more than ephemeral — before you know it, it's over.

Blessedly, mercifully over.

2. LET'S GET SEXIST

There are physiological differences between men and women.

I'll pause here a moment while you gasp.

OK, I'll admit that this is no great revelation to anyone reading this. Nevertheless, anytime it's pointed out — in any way besides the undeniable broad statement I just made — people seem to get very upset or uncomfortable.

That's because our belief in equality is so strong that whenever any differences between the genders are pointed out — beyond the obvious anatomical ones — we feel the statement must be sexist.

But the plain fact is that only women can get pregnant. Even this fact causes many of us to bristle. In our language, we even try to ignore this fact, as though the mere admission or mention of it is no longer politically correct. How many times have you heard a couple say, "We're pregnant"?

The truth is "we" are not pregnant. "We" are not getting morning sickness. "Our" boobs are not getting bigger. And "we" are not going to push a seven-pound sack of human flesh through "our" vaginas.

"She" however, will do all those things.

But just as there are physical differences, there are chemical and hormonal differences; which means there are emotional differences.

And if you follow that line of thought to its logical conclusion, the way a woman experiences pregnancy, birth, infancy and toddlerhood are necessarily different from the way a man experiences these things.

While both men and women cry when they're sad, I think men are more likely to cry when they get choked up than women are.

Again, I know that's a generalization. I know men who love babies. I know women who can't stand them.

I have a sister whose maternal instinct is so strong it was obvious from her own toddlerhood that she would make a great mother — so strong it led her to a career as an EMT and a nurse.

My other sister has the maternal instinct of a praying mantis, and it led her to a career in web design.

But this book isn't for women.

In our society, women are encouraged to explore their emotions. It's acceptable. It's healthy. It makes you live longer.

Men are encouraged to stifle their emotions, pushing them further and further down with greater and greater pressure until they come exploding to the surface like a 6-megaton bomb. And that's a shame.

I truly believe that men and women experience the same emotions to the same degree. But I also believe those emotions tend to manifest themselves differently.

For example, while both men and women cry when they're sad, I think men are more likely to cry when they get choked up than women are.

Women, on the other hand, are more likely to cry when they're angry. Men very rarely cry when they're angry. They're more likely to hit things. And we don't want men to hit things — especially when they have a child in their care.

So it's a good idea to find a better outlet for that particular emotion. And the best way to control an emotion, I believe, is to be prepared for it.

Now, I'm no psychologist or sociologist. I'm not an expert in parenting, child welfare or child development.

I'm just a dad.

I'm twice divorced and am now happily married to my third wife. I have a child with each of my ex-wives, and there's one on the way with my current wife.

Circumstances led me to where I am in life right now. But the situation has also given me a unique way of looking at things. I not only know what pregnancy and child-rearing are like, I know what they're like with different types of women.

I also know now what to be prepared for.

Let me fill you in ...

3. PREPARE TO BE PREPARED

It will indeed be a wonderful moment when your wife gleefully shows you the double-line on the stick she just peed all over. But you have to understand, that is by no means the beginning of the story. No, no, no.

You see, once you and your wife or fiancée or girlfriend or whatever decide you want to have a child — well, that's when the adventure begins. There are many things you will experience then that you may not be prepared for.

Now you will be.

First, if your wife is on the pill, she will stop taking the pill and her body will make itself a nice comfortable place for a fetus to gestate. The nice thing is that her body will do this all on its own. You don't have to do anything. She doesn't have to do anything.

That doesn't mean, however, that there won't be repercussions.

You see, if your wife has been on the pill for a long time, the transition back to a non-pill cycle may not be as flawless and unnoticeable as you're anticipating. She may have forgotten that she gets moody, or crampy, or has a heavy flow, or has an irregular cycle, or bursts into tears when you make a comment about the weather.

She may experience none of these things. Or — God help the both of you — she may experience all of them. This is the first thing you need to prepare for. One thing is certain: being a man, you won't have to experience any of these things, but you will experience the effects of them.

The only thing you can do is be understanding. Your instinct may be to point out to your wife how ridiculous it is to have a meltdown over the fact that you've run out of orange juice.

Do *not* do this. Simply hug her and tell her everything is OK. And for God's sake, go out and get more orange juice. Whatever you do, don't let it devolve into an argument. It will leave you both angry and confused and having no idea why. This is all easily avoided.

If your wife is well prepared, she may have already consulted with her gynecologist, who may have prescribed prenatal vitamins. These are a wonderful thing that will help your wife's body prepare itself for conception.

They will also make it difficult for her to poop.

This may lead to more moodiness, cramps, etc.

Now, you may be lucky enough to hit the pregnancy target on the first try. If you do, good for you; that means you won't have to endure this next part: baby envy.

Your wife may cry and be depressed when she gets her period when she was hoping for egg fertilization. Again, be there to comfort her. But there's something else you need to be ready for. Suddenly — and I can't stress enough that this is an inevitability — every woman you know or run across will be pregnant or holding a baby. Seriously, you two won't be able to sit down in a café without a pregnant woman standing in line behind you, or a newborn baby at the table next to yours.

This will make your wife angry, because she wants a baby. And she wants one now. You will find yourself awkwardly and quietly enumerating to your wife the reasons why she cannot steal the baby she sees. You will have to explain to her that it doesn't matter if the baby's mother has turned her back for a moment.

But it's unavoidable. There will be babies everywhere. And Facebook has just exacerbated this problem. Your wife's newsfeed will be filled with pictures of smiling babies. Even better, mothers-to-be will post photos of their latest sonogram, because apparently they want the whole world to see exactly what's going on in their wombs.

As a side note, your wife will say to you, "When I'm pregnant, don't let me post a photo of my sonogram. I don't want to be one of *those* kinds of mothers." Good luck holding her to that. You may want to get it in writing. Maybe even get it notarized.

Finally and most importantly, in order for her to get pregnant, you're going to have to have sex. And your wife may not understand why saying things like, "Let's make a baby," or "Make me a mommy" doesn't turn you on. You may try to compensate by being a little naughtier than usual. This will upset her. She will wonder why you would be the slightest bit prurient when you're doing something as wholesome as manufacturing human life — as though the baby were already there and you were having sex right in front of it.

This will stress her out. It will stress you out. You will both be so stressed out you may find it impossible to conceive.

Unlike baby envy, this is easy to avoid. Simply talk about it. I don't mean you should broach the subject mid-foreplay. I mean you should sit down and discuss it. Maybe even read her this passage, and then she may understand where you're coming from.

Maybe she'll even dress up as a cheerleader or something.

While you've been very understanding about all those other things, your wife may find herself in a position where she has to be understanding for once.

Fair is fair.

4. GETTING STUFF

When you have a baby, you're going to need a lot of stuff: cribs, changing tables, car seats, high chairs, carriages, strollers, those weird little flying saucer things they bounce around in, diaper bags, breast pumps, and those little blue bulbs to suck boogers out of their nose. Unless you're independently wealthy, there's no way for you to pay for all this stuff. But fret not. Our society has devised a way for you to show up at one event where people will give you all of this and more.

Now, much has been written about baby showers and their place in our culture. Nobody likes them.

Nobody likes hosting them. Nobody likes attending them.

But alas, you cannot just contact your family and friends and say, "Hey! Give me stuff!" That would be vulgar. You instead have to make them sit through an agonizingly tedious event where you ooh and aah over gifts you already know you're getting because you filled out the baby registry at your local department store.

There was a time when the father's role in this ritual was limited to getting the mother-to-be to the venue on time while maintaining the surprise. Because just as she has to be surprised by gifts she already knows she's getting, apparently she also has to be surprised by an event she already knows is taking place. It seems to me to be ludicrous, but who am I to meddle with the wisdom of the natal gods.

Anyway, as I said, the father's role was one of getting the mother to the event and then leaving. Later on, you would also have to carry all those things home and put them together with a tiny little Allen wrench.

Today, you still have to do all these things, but you might be expected to stay for the baby shower, too. Other men may be invited. It will probably take place on a Sunday around brunch time. The invitees will consist of excited grandparents-to-be, a whole lot of women who look bored and uncomfortable, men who keep looking at their watches because there's a football game today, and old ladies sucking down mimosas to make the whole experience tolerable. Have fun.

Next, you have to get all these things home, unless you had the luck or foresight to have this shower in your own home. If not, get ready to carry stuff. Depending on how many people you invited, you may want to rent a U-Haul.

Now, somewhere during the pregnancy, your wife will experience what is called nesting.

I once had some pet mice that I thought were three females. It turns out that they were two females and a male. I found this out when one of the mice became pregnant. After removing the male (for fear that it would eat its offspring) I watched with fascination while the two remaining females made nests with whatever cardboard, straw, or anything else I threw in their cage. They chewed up stuff, kept stuff, threw some stuff away, all with such amazing speed and agility it left me bewildered.

After the baby mice were born, they started doing it again, building a new nest. I was perplexed, but then watched with fascination as they took turns carrying the baby mice from the old nest to the new one.

Now, I have no idea what was wrong with the old nest, or what was so great about the new one. But then, I'm not a mouse. I know this because a gym teacher once asked me, "Are you a man or a mouse?" I meekly answered, "man," and he told me I was right. That's how I know.

Anyway, the reason I share that little anecdote with you is that I want you to picture it, but with people (except for the part about the male eating the baby. You probably won't do that.)

The nesting instinct is a strong one. And when I say "strong" I mean that in a very literal way. I actually came home one time to find my wife had thrown a whole recliner off the back deck. And we were living in a second-floor apartment at the time. It seems that her instinct told her this piece of furniture was no longer welcome in our home and just had to go — immediately. Rather than wait for me, she decided (or rather her instinct decided) to do it all on her own, and she heaved that chair over the deck railing with an incredible strength for which I would not have given her credit. Such is the strength of motherhood.

So the thing to take away from this is that you may be making way for a new baby, but it's your wife's way your going to want to stay clear of — or you might just find a recliner falling from the sky.

5. STANDARD DELIVERY

In William Shakespeare's "Macbeth," the title character remains cocky and fearless, even while his enemies pile up at the front door. That's because a few witches told him he could never be defeated "by a man of woman born."

Well, every man is born of woman; so, he concludes, nobody can defeat him. But when he's in his final scene going tête-à-tête with his nemesis, Macduff, he learns an important fact from the lips of the man himself: "Macduff was from his mother's womb untimely ripped."

For those of us who have been in the delivery room, that word "ripped" takes on a special meaning.

Obviously, Macduff came into the world through some sort of medieval C-section.

No matter how your baby comes into the world, either standard delivery or untimely ripped from his mother's womb, you'll be there to witness it — unless you're deployed overseas. Gone are the days when fathers paced around the waiting room or, in my father's case, dropped their wives off at the front door of the hospital, then went off for a round of golf.

No, you'll be right there to witness and share every beautiful, miraculous and incredibly gory second of it.

Both ways, caesarean section and vaginal delivery, are fraught with adventure. And I ought to know, I've witnessed both. For my daughter, it was the traditional route. This is the one area where I know you've already been warned, so I'll avoid all the clichéd jokes that seem to abound in delivery room scenes in film and television.

What I will say is this: I used to think there was nothing stranger than hearing an angry priest yelling a string of obscenities (yes, I've witnessed this). Now I know that there is something stranger: hearing an angry obstetrician yell a string of obscenities.

First, let me set the stage for you.

You see, the people in my family are genetically predisposed to big-headedness. We are a large-headed people. I'm not talking circus-freak large or anything — just a lot of plus-sized craniums. I like to tell myself that I store an awful lot of knowledge in there and it's simply a matter of capacity.

Anyway, my children inherited the big-headed gene.

So, my daughter just couldn't seem to squeeze her head out into daylight. The doctor, who said, "All right, we're not trying to win any records for longest labor ever here," tried every tool at his disposal: drugs, salad tongs, suction cups (I'm sure there's medical terminology for these things, but in my traumatized state I didn't bother to ask).

These things didn't work. And they so angered the obstetrician, that he actually threw the suction cup thing across the delivery room. Eventually, though, the baby made its appearance.

There is one thing that they may not warn you about ahead of time. When your baby is delivered vaginally, it won't look the way newborns look in the movies. Its head will have the shape, color and texture of a weathered traffic cone. Do not panic. This is only temporary.

It was a different story with my son. For reasons of safety, she elected for a C-section, This was a completely different type of adventure — one where you'll get to dress up like a surgeon.

My wife wasn't completely knocked out, but she was so pumped up with silly juice that she was unable to form words. I don't know where she thought she was, because I couldn't understand her.

They'll seat you right next to her head so you can whisper encouraging things to her. Whether any of these things register is anybody's bet. There will be a cloth between her head and the rest of her, so you can't really see what's going on. That is, until the moment arrives.

They'll ask you if you want to witness the miracle of your baby being pulled through the gash they just sliced in your wife's belly. You'll have to decide whether or not you can handle it. There is a lot of blood. We're talking zombie-movie gore here.

But I decided I couldn't pass it up and that my stomach was strong enough to endure whatever the doctors were wrist deep in.

Fortunately, I was correct.

How can I describe what it was like seeing my son for the first time? You know that scene in "Alien" when the creature forces its way out of John Hurt's chest? Well, it was just like that, except the baby looked angrier.

Then they'll ask you if you want to cut the cord. I didn't want to cut the cord.

I'm guessing most fathers do for some reason, because they were surprised. Then they were insistent, even after I explained that I had no interest. Maybe they thought that if I didn't I would be living with the worst kind of regret for the rest of my life.

But I did get to hold him as soon as they finished all the medical stuff they had to do.

Since he was a boy, a decision had to be made: would he be circumcised? For such a personal decision, you'll be surprised how many of your family and friends want to weigh in on it.

The more verbose and opinionated will tell you that there's no medical reason for it — that if you allow it to happen, you'll be guilty of mutilation. Others will tell you that you should do it so he's not different from the other boys in the locker room (although I don't recall ever examining the anatomy of other guys when I was in the locker room.)

My sister, who's a nurse, regaled me with horrifying tales of old uncircumcised men.

But the clincher came from a friend who said she would always have her sons circumcised. She said, "No son of mine is going to go through life with an ugly man-unit."

Now that's an argument ender if ever there was one.

6. YOUR NEWBORN IS DISGUSTING

As your new baby is presented to loved ones for the very first time, you will hear the following sentences uttered by the baby's mother, grandmothers, sisters and aunts:

"She's so beautiful!"

"Oh my God! So adorable I could just eat her up!"

"She looks just like her mother."

"She looks just like her father."

"She is the loveliest thing I've ever seen!"

You will look at the baby and think she looks just like Winston Churchill stepping out of a particularly long and unproductive bath.

Also, your newborn smells really bad.

I can hear a lot of women reading the previous sentence and shouting, "No, it doesn't! I love new baby smell!"

But this isn't addressed to women. It's addressed to fathers.

You see, there's something in a woman's hormones, hypothalamus or hard-wiring that makes them believe newborns smell divine.

I've even witnessed the disquieting sight of a roomful of women passing an infant around to sniff. Each one will put the baby's head right up to her nose and inhale deeply, like a stoner taking a hit from a joint.

It seems so enticing. And the peer pressure will be so overwhelming that you'll find yourself sticking the baby's head in front of your face and taking a big whiff.

Do not do this.

To a new father — unequipped with the maternal nose filter that renders all babies sweet-smelling — your new baby will smell like a mixture of vinegar and low tide.

Seriously, think of the things that routinely force themselves out of your body. How many of them smell good? There's no reason to believe a baby will be any different.

Should you find yourself in the situation I've just described, under no circumstances should you let any women know that this baby is an assault on your nostrils. They will be unforgiving in their hostility.

And the bad smell doesn't end there.

The first time you change a newborn's diaper, you'll encounter this black, viscous substance that looks like it should be used to blacktop a driveway. Oddly enough, it won't smell. That's because it's not real poop. It's something called meconium. It's waste left over from the baby's time in the womb. It's disgusting to look at but relatively odorless.

Don't let this lull you into a false sense of security!

Before long, the baby will begin pooping real poop.

Now I've smelled all kinds of waste — human, cow, dog — all with varying degrees of offensiveness. But I assure you, all the scented candles, aerosol sprays and air fresheners in the world will not cloak the stench that will encircle you for the next year or so.

And if you opt for formula instead of breastfeeding, you may find that what goes into your baby can smell just as bad as what comes out.

When my daughter was an infant, we had to ditch the Enfamil and start using something called Nutramigen. It's packed with all sorts of ingredients to make digestion easier for your baby and ease colic.

It also smells like Michael Flatley's footbath.

But it's not all bad.

Once the baby is sitting up — usually around six months — you can start giving it baby food. Try the peaches. The peaches are the best. And the reason they're the best is that they actually make your baby's breath smell good.

It's a small reward you'll appreciate greatly after so many months with this fetid creature in your home.

In the meantime, what you may want to do is keep a bag of coffee beans handy, like they do in scented candle shops. When you need to, stick your face in it just to reset your olfactory nerve.

7. FRAGILE: HANDLE WITH CARE

W hat's the difference between a baby and a cast-iron pan? The cast-iron pan is more likely to break. I'm not even kidding. The first time you pick up your baby, you'll probably be terrified that you're going to do something wrong and crush it like Lenny in "Of Mice and Men."

But fret not. Nature has designed babies so that they can endure all sorts of clumsy idiots. Don't get me wrong, I'm not advocating that you toss your baby around like a football. I'm just saying they're not the delicate flowers many believe them to be.

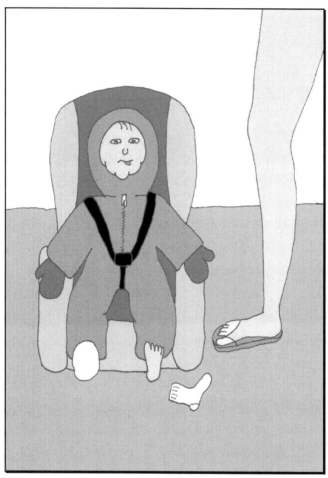

For some reason, older people are terrified that babies are going to freeze to death and insist on wrapping them up in layers — even on a hot summer's day.

It's important to know this, because you'll encounter a lot of people out there who'll be horrified by the way you hold, touch or dress your baby. And some new parents are so crazy about this — particularly with their firstborns — that they'll insist you not touch their child unless you've sterilized your hands by plunging them into boiling water.

The best way to deal with these people is to humor them. You'll find many who — and this is especially true for old people — are convinced your baby is too cold. For some reason, older people are terrified that babies are going to freeze to death and insist on wrapping them up in layers — even on a hot summer's day. Every pediatrician I've spoken to on this subject tells me the same thing: if you're cold, your baby is cold. If you're hot, your baby is hot.

While this seems to make perfect sense, you may encounter some grandparents who will quickly dismiss this logic as the worst kind of nonsense. Apparently, they know better: your baby is a shivering pile of misery that needs more layers.

Another thing you'll hear about is "the soft spot." This is just the part of the head where the plates of the skull have not yet fused into one solid bone. It's called the fontanel, and despite its folksier moniker, it's about as soft and delicate as an old catcher's mitt. I once had an old lady scream, "Watch the soft spot!" at me as I was slipping a knit cap over my daughter's head. I don't know what she thought this hat of yarn was going to do to her, but by the way she was ranting, you'd think a misplaced cap would cause a cranial chain reaction that would eventually keep my daughter out of the best universities.

There are also those who get really upset when they see a baby outside. The reason is that they're convinced the baby will get a cold or "catch something" if it's allowed outdoors. I don't know why these people believe the stagnant, disease-ridden air of the average home is somehow safer than the fresh air of the great outdoors. Again, I think there's a conventional wisdom that your baby just isn't tough enough to handle the weather.

As your baby gets older and starts to try standing up and walking, it's going to fall down — a lot. When this happens, terrified adults (yourself included) will come swooping in to cradle and comfort the baby in addition to checking for injuries. There will probably be no injuries.

Soon, every time your toddler falls, it will immediately look at you to decide whether or not it should start crying. If the baby thinks you didn't notice, it will go about its business. If it sees you making a fuss or showing concern, it will wail uncontrollably. When my kids were at that age, I used to look away and pretend I didn't see anything whenever they fell, just so I could avoid listening to a 10-minute crying jag.

Sometimes others would be horrified by this — particularly women, even after I demonstrated the truth of what I was saying. I think the maternal instinct is so strong to rush to the baby's aid, that something as weak as pure logic is not enough to overpower it.

So baby pratfalls usually go this way: baby falls, daddy ignores it, baby is fine. Or baby falls, mommy swoops in to comfort baby, baby cries for 10 minutes. Just watch, you'll find out I'm right.

Sometimes, when new mothers bring a baby home, they want the baby to sleep in the same room as mommy and daddy. The reason for this is mommies are terrified they'll fall into such a deep slumber that they won't hear their baby screaming for food in the next room. The reality is that if mommy were sleeping in one wing of Buckingham Palace and the baby were sleeping in the other wing, mommy would wake up and come running if the baby said "peep."

So my advice is to save money on the basinet (had one once, used it once) and let your kid get used to the crib. Don't let it sleep in your bed. For one thing, you can roll over and suffocate it.

For another thing, it will identify your bed as a place of comfort and refuge and never want to leave — ever. I knew one couple whose 5-year-old son was still sleeping with them every night because mommy couldn't bear the thought of the boy sleeping all alone. That'll probably get pretty awkward by the time the kid is 13.

Just relax, trust your instincts and learn to tune out those people who tell you you're doing everything wrong. Just treat your baby gently as you would any other living thing and it may just survive to adulthood.

8. THE WONDERFUL WORLD OF POOP

You may have gone your entire life up to this point without ever having considered poop. You may never truly have pondered its complexities, its value, yes, even its ramifications.

Well, that all changes immediately. Because from now on, you're wrist-deep in it, my friend.

And I know what you're thinking. You're thinking, yeah, yeah, I know all about the fact that I'm going to be changing a lot of smelly diapers. That's true, but you're kidding yourself if you believe it begins and ends with that.

Yes, changing diapers will become a big part of your life. And yes, there are times when you will wonder aloud how it's possible for such a small child to poop out half its body weight. But here's some stuff you may not know.

You don't have to wait for the unmistakable odor of baby waste to know what's about to happen. You will find there are other clues that a baby is about to crap itself.

Most subtle is what I call "the poop stare."

It doesn't matter what he or she is doing: smiling, laughing, crying or cooing; suddenly, time will freeze and your child's face will go completely blank. He or she will adopt the same vacant, meaningless expression of a man who's been standing in line way too long at the DMV. This means your baby is engaged in the act of pooping. As far as warnings go, this one isn't particularly helpful, since it's just a matter of seconds between blank expression and the noxious fumes of the soiled diaper.

But in those circumstances where every second counts — for instance in a crowded restaurant where patrons probably don't want to experience your baby's foulness — it may give you just enough of a window to whisk your offensive child downwind of your fellow diners.

As far as your own home goes, however, the smell will linger like gunpowder on the Fourth of July. But there are ways to deal with it, thanks to the technological advances of our age. I am referring to the Diaper Genie.

This little gem is merely a high-tech diaper pail. Inside is a long tubular plastic bag. All you have to do is quickly shove the dirty diaper into it, give it a twist, and the odor is safely locked away in a tiny airtight prison. This is a wonderful invention that will save you from vomit-inducing fumes — until it comes time to empty it out.

When this thing gets full — and believe me, you'll put it off by stuffing diapers in it until it's ready to explode — you'll have to take it outside and dump it. What will come spilling out resembles the biggest, foulest sausage links in the world. And despite that it's airtight, these diapers have been fermenting inside their tubular Petri dish for a while. Your garbage man will hate you.

But your poop experiences won't be confined to the diaper and changing table. For even though you try to keep your baby's butt safely covered, like a bottle of nitroglycerin that could explode on its own any moment, there are times when that's just not possible. One of those times is while the child is taking a bath.

I'm not saying this will happen to you, but once, while I was giving my son a bath (long after he had mastered sitting up on his own), my attention was diverted for no more than a second. It was enough time for him to poop. Clearly, while washing him I had neglected to see the tell-tale blank stare, because the next thing I knew, the boy was playing with it like it was his new favorite bath toy. I don't want to get into the disgusting physical description of a waterlogged baby turd. Suffice to say, it was an unpleasant experience that left me on edge in the bathtub worse than the shower scene from "Psycho."

The last thing I need to warn you about is poop obsession. I don't know how common this is, but I've known at least a couple of women who insist on a detailed daily report about the quality of their baby's poop. I mean they want to know the size, shape, color and consistency of everything that comes out of their child's backside.

I assume there's some book out there that suggests to new mothers that poop is the very best barometer to a baby's health, though I can honestly say I've never had a pediatrician ask me, "So how does the poop look?"

In any event, I created a poop classification system. The different categories are 'musket ball,' 'volcano,' 'tar', 'mud patty,' 'Yule log,' and the rare but disturbing 'baseball.'

I don't know if any of this will be of help to you, but there it is.

9. SHRIEKING AND OTHER FORMS OF COMMUNICATION

When a baby forces its way out of the womb and first hits the cold fresh air, the very first thing it does is communicate its feelings to whoever happens to be there. This takes the form of an ear-splitting shriek that could rend the very heavens.

The shrieking is not their fault. Imagine if you were warm and comfortable in your bed and suddenly someone decided to bring you out into the cold night air by pulling you through a tiny hole in the wall. That's right — you'd shriek too.

During your baby's first year, it will have a lot of new thoughts it wants to communicate: it's hungry, it's tired, it's happy, it's sad, it's gassy, it's hot, it's cold, it's uncomfortable, it's scared, it's awake, it's wet, its diaper is full of poop, or it's getting really, really sick of breast milk. All of these thoughts will take the form of a loud, shrill cry.

If you go to childbirth classes — and I suggest you do because they not only teach your wife how to breathe, they also teach you how not to kill your new baby — one of the things they usually do is play a recording of a baby crying for one minute straight. They do this to show new parents just how long a minute can be when it's spent with an infant who's wailing like a World War II air raid siren. I suspect they also scan the crowd to see if it causes any parents-to-be to look like they want to kill someone.

Unfortunately, there's no way of knowing which of the things listed above your baby is trying to communicate, so you'll try each one of them until you hit the target.

You'll check the diaper — it'll be dry. You'll try the bottle — he won't want it. You'll try to burp it — nothing will come out. After running through the entire baby-distress checklist, you'll be at your wit's end as to what exactly this baby is crying about. Right around this time, the baby will stop crying for no apparent reason.

After gaining enough experience, you'll be able to distinguish one type of cry from another. You'll amaze your friends by saying things like, "Oh, that's a tired cry if ever I've heard one." Eventually, you'll say this with the confidence of a wine connoisseur who can identify a particular vintage just by sniffing it: "Ah, now this one has the full-body tones of a hungry cry, but I detect the subtle-yet-playful undercurrent of a poopy cry as well."

In any event, you should prepare yourself for the screaming. I don't know exactly how to do that — maybe press your ear against the hood of your car after triggering the alarm — I don't know. But that's what your baby is going to sound like for the first year whenever it's awake.

I once had to watch my infant niece for a couple of hours while my sister was out running errands. The girl screamed for two hours straight, pausing only once to vomit.

I don't want to stereotype all babies here. Not all of them scream constantly. I once spent an hour in a restaurant with a conscious and alert baby at the next table who didn't make a peep the entire time it was there. There is no way this was a normal baby. Clearly the parents had drugged it with some sort of opiate compound. And I don't approve of that sort of thing.

Eventually, your baby will learn a few non-shrieking forms of communication. One of the earliest is sign language. Apparently it's easier for babies to sign than speak. Touching the hand to the chin to say "more" seems to be a favorite among infants and parents alike.

Finally, the day will come when your baby will make an intelligible sound. That sound will be "dada." This will infuriate your wife, who — as far as she is concerned — carried around that precious little bundle for nine months, and if it's going to start talking now it sure as hell better say "mama."

Be ready to talk her down by explaining to her that it's just a lot easier for babies to form the sound "dada" than "mama." Or if you're more sadistic, explain to her that the baby has already chosen its favorite and she lost out.

This is one of the greatest joys of child development. Soon your baby will be making not only sounds, but words. And not just ordinary words, but cute words; like saying "brefkis" when they mean "breakfast."

Soon those words will become sentences and your baby will discover literary devices such as metaphor, irony and onomatopoeia.

Those sentences will quickly turn into questions, and you will find you've become your toddler's go-to reference for every single question it has about the world — a virtual encyclopedia with an answer to every question from "how does water come out of that faucet?" to "why is that car blue?"

And before you know it, your little bundle of joy will be tattling to mommy that you fed him hot dogs for dinner three nights in a row, or how you flirted with that blond barista in the coffee shop.

Before long, you'll be looking back fondly on those days when your kid would just scream like a banshee when he had something to say.

10. ADVENTURES IN EATING

It has been said that there are three things that can never be done to the satisfaction of everyone in the room: stoking a fire, managing a baseball team and burping a baby.

Now, when a baby is very little, it's important to support its head. I've been told this by a number of people every single time I pick up an infant, that's how I know it's true.

Apparently, if you don't support its head, it'll just snap off and roll across the floor.

So, make sure that head is firmly in place when it comes time to burp the baby. And make sure you drape a cloth over your shoulder. This is because baby burps tend to be half gas, half liquid.

It doesn't matter what amount of force you use to pat the baby's back, because no matter how you do it, you're doing it wrong. There will always be some woman in the room to tell you you're doing it wrong and insist that you pass the baby over. Either you'll be patting it too hard or not hard enough. It will never be just right. In all my years, I have never hit the Goldilocks spot of baby burping — at least not according to any woman who has witnessed my attempts.

As the child gets a little older and its head is no longer two-thirds the size of its body, it will be able to support its cranium all on its own. This is good, because it allows you a safer burping position. Safe for you, I mean.

You see, as a baby gets older, the danger of spit-up increases exponentially. So does the amount of spit-up. So I like to hold the child face downward away from me while I'm patting its back. Women are horrified by this. But I don't care; at least I'm away from any milky puke that comes exploding out of the baby's mouth. I swear to God, sometimes it seems like a quart.

No matter what, you'll be surrounded by people who tell you you're holding, burping, changing, even looking at the baby in the wrong way. It's a good idea to humor these people. They're nuts.

Then the day will come — usually around six months — when your baby can sit up. Praise this day. It means that you can now put it in a high chair. But this is both good news and bad news. It's good because you no longer have to constantly carry and hold your baby while it's eating, burping, etc. It's bad because the high chair and the floor surrounding it will become the filthiest place in your home. Green, mushy baby food will dry and cement itself to any surface more efficiently than an industrial bonding agent. A fine dust of Cheerio crumbs will cover everything in a three-foot radius. Everything will be sticky.

One thing I was never forewarned about was the mock-choking panic. It has happened to me with every baby, yet I've never heard anyone else mention it. At some point, while feeding your child, it will suddenly look very surprised and its eyes will start bugging out. It looks like the child is choking; this will cause your heart to sink and your stomach to flip. You may even soil yourself. You will pry open your baby's mouth in a vain attempt to yank out whatever is in there.

Then you will remember your baby is eating mush. You'll look back at your baby's eyes, which now look completely normal, except that they may look back at you quizzically, no doubt wondering why you just shoved your fingers in its mouth.

I'm sure you've already been told by many sources what to do in a real choking emergency. Thankfully, I have never been in one of these situations. And I would like to keep it that way. The false alarms were traumatic enough.

As your child ages, it will fit in neatly to one of three eating categories.

The first is the child that will eat anything put in front of it, with very little preference. If you have such a child, consider yourself fortunate. My son is in this category. I could give him a small dish of M&Ms or a small dish of peas. He would eat both with the same level of contentment. I should have known right off the bat that he would be this way, since when he was an infant his favorite food was whatever he happened to find on the floor.

When he was about two years old, I was making us dinner one night. He was seated in his high chair when I began bringing dishes of food to the table — family style. The first thing I brought was a bowl of broccoli. Apparently he didn't know that this was a side for both of us to share, because when I returned with the next side, the bowl was empty. He had completely devoured the entire broccoli I had made. He must have assumed that that was his dinner.

The second type of child is the one who has identified certain foods it likes and will consume nothing else. My daughter used to fit into this category when she was a toddler. She eventually grew out of it, but for a while there I feared she would go through her whole life eating nothing but pancakes and macaroni & cheese.

The third type of child is the one who has never eaten the tiniest morsel of food without being coaxed, cajoled, bribed, blackmailed or threatened. This type of child is particularly frustrating for grandparents who, for some reason, seem to derive much of their joy from seeing their grandchildren eat. You can tell they just want to scream at the child sitting at the dinner table who's unwillingly eating one molecule of food per minute.

I have never had such a child, but I have seen them. If you wind up with one of these, good luck.

11. COMING LATE TO THE POTTY

Some day, your child may pilot a fighter jet, captain an aircraft carrier, preside over the United Nations, or conquer Mount Everest. But before any of that happens, he or she will have to become adept at using the toilet. It's a prerequisite for all of those things — I checked.

This is one of those developmental things that doesn't happen at a specific time. The reason I know this is because my older sister was toilet trained at 18 months — a fact my mother has bragged about ceaselessly. I, on the other hand, didn't make friends with the commode until the ripe old age of 3½ — a fact my mother mentions often with a disappointed shake of the head, as though it's something that should still fill me with shame.

You've probably heard the sexist generalization that girls are a lot easier to toilet train than boys. Well, I'm here to set the record straight and tell you that's absolutely, 100% true. My daughter picked up her mastery of the toilet so quickly it's all still a blur. My son, on the other hand was either unwilling or unable, so it became a bone of contention between us.

I tried everything with that kid: rushing him to the toilet when he pooped, offering rewards, and even giving him his own little toilet that would play a little musical flourish when he peed in it. One day I actually heard the little potty music and ran into the bathroom in a state of uncontrolled excitement. It turns out the little dear had actually figured out a way to make the toilet play music by jury-rigging the bottom of it. OK, maybe he'll be an engineer some day, I thought, but not till he masters this pooping thing.

OK, he was only 2½ at the time, but it was nonetheless beginning to be a problem, because as I may have mentioned before, my son was enormous. I don't mean he was fat; actually he was quite proportional. But he was extremely tall, so he was always the size he should be if he were at least a year older. I actually had to throw away all the newborn onesies I bought because he would only fit in 3-6 months-sized immediately after birth. But I'm starting to ramble.

The point is that he was already wearing the largest diapers that were commercially available (for babies) and I wanted him to come to terms with the toilet as quickly as possible before I had a full-blown crisis on my hands.

Since toilet training for a boy is a specialty, I resolved to contact one of the many young mothers I knew at the time to enlist her help. The older mothers I spoke to just didn't remember exactly how they did it, probably because they blocked the whole agonizing process from their minds. Unfortunately, every young mother I knew — without exception — was raising a girl.

That's great for the boy, I thought. He'll have his pick of women when he gets older, but that hardly helps me now.

So I turned to the greatest source of modern knowledge I could find: Facebook. It was in the early days of the cultural phenomenon, and I had just friended several old classmates from elementary school, one of whom had a son about the same age as mine.

Now, keep in mind that I hadn't said hello to this woman in 25 years. We got reacquainted by my asking her how to get my son to stop crapping in his diaper. To my grateful astonishment, she responded with paragraph after paragraph of detail.

If you had told me in 1986 that this girl I barely ever spoke to would one day send me her potty-training manifesto with the click of a button, I never would have believed you — mostly because computers at that time could do little more than make dot matrix banners on those long sheets of paper with the little holes in the side.

Anyway, she told me to pick a day when I could keep the boy at home in whatever room he plays in. All I had to do was stick his little toilet in the room and have him go pantless and diaperless. It seemed a little odd, but I was at the end of my rope. Sure enough, it worked on the first try.

So now he's free to pursue a life of adventure and intellectual fulfillment. But none of it would have been possible if not for his mastery of the porcelain conundrum.

I hope he remembers to thank me for it during his Nobel Prize acceptance speech.

12. BATHROOM ETIQUETTE

When my daughter was almost 2 years old, I had a work schedule that left me alone with her during the day while my wife was at work. During this time, she was my responsibility — and mine alone. At that age, you don't want to leave your child by herself for a moment. Still there are certain things you have to do that require your attention to be elsewhere.

That's where the television comes in.

I know, I know. It's terrible; you shouldn't use Barney as a babysitter, blah blah blah.

But it was nice to know that I could put my daughter in a trance for half an hour while I shaved, took a shower, and attended to the rest of my toilette.

And so this became a ritual. I would plop her in front of the TV and hop into the shower.

Realizing that between the sound of the running water and the bathroom vent, I would never hear my daughter if something happened to her, I used to keep the door ajar — just in case Barney jumped out of the television set and started strangling her.

This worked fine for a while, until one day when I was shampooing and suddenly felt a cold draft. You know, the kind you get when the shower curtain isn't fully closed.

I didn't think much of it until I heard a tiny little voice say, "Daddy! You have a tail!"

I guess she got bored with Barney. And who could really blame her?

But that's just the sort of thing none of the parenting books prepared me for.

But it's important to me that you, the new father, be ready for these little surprises.

And the bathroom holds many — particularly public restrooms.

When he couldn't find anything to wipe himself with, he decided to hop over to one of the toilet stalls — with his pants around his ankles — in a futile quest for some toilet paper.

Before any woman anywhere exits a bathroom, some sort of wiping will have taken place. This is an obvious anatomical necessity. Men, on the other hand, rely on the shake.

When my son was being toilet trained, every woman involved in the process insisted on teaching him to wipe himself after peeing.

That's not necessary, I insisted. Men don't do that. "Well, they should!" said the various women with their faces wrinkled up in disgusted grimaces. "It's neater and more sanitary."

Granted. I have no doubt it is more sanitary. But I also remember what I was told when I was a little boy: "No matter how much you shake, wiggle or dance, the last couple of drops end up in your pants."

Who am I to argue with the wisdom of poetry?

But again, these women only take their own experiences into consideration. What they don't realize is that urinals in public men's rooms do not have toilet paper — or anything else whereby you can wipe yourself. And so it came to pass that I was in the men's room with my son at a movie theater when we shared a pee break at the movie's conclusion.

He had been taught by his mother to wipe.

Now I didn't have a clear view of him, because I was at a grown-up urinal and he was at one of the little boy urinals.

But when he couldn't find anything to wipe himself with, he decided to hop over to one of the toilet stalls — with his pants around his ankles — in a futile quest for some toilet paper. Alas, all the stalls were occupied, so he just bounced up and down half naked. I'm fairly certain all that naked jumping around rendered the need of toilet paper moot. But he was insistent.

I had to explain to him that, despite what mommy, grandma, auntie or any other woman might tell him, he doesn't have to worry about wiping after peeing.

You may want to have this same conversation with your own son — preferably someplace a little more private than a crowded public restroom.

13. HIDDEN BENEFITS

When you have a kid, you're going to get a lot of advice from a lot of people. Usually these things are dire warnings about how much your life will change. You will be warned about lack of sleep. You will be warned about finances. You will be warned about how you'll never have fun ever again. You will be told that everything is different now — that you will be worrying about this child from now until the day you die.

What they usually don't tell you is all the many benefits that go along with raising a child. I don't mean intangibles like, "It's the most rewarding thing you can ever do." No, I'm talking about real benefits here.

The first benefit is the excuse. This begins with pregnancy. Your wife will find herself saying something like, "Sorry I'm late, the baby kept me up late last night with nausea, etc."

After the baby is born, you will continue doing that. A pregnant woman or new parent never has to show up on time for anything. All you have to do is blame the baby. You're late because the baby has colic. You have to leave early because it's time for the baby's nap. It can't speak for itself, so there's nothing it can do about your filthy lies. This brings us to our next benefit: blame.

While you can use the baby as an excuse for anything, it doesn't stop there. What's that awful smell? Must be the baby. I guess the little tyke is really gassy today. You can be flatulent with impunity. Nobody has to know that the baby is innocent — that what they smell is really the burrito you had for lunch. Again, the baby can't defend itself. Besides, the day will come when it gets its vindication. One of the first sentences a child ever utters is "That wasn't me, that was Daddy!" It comes soon enough, so enjoy blaming the kid now while you can. And do it guilt free.

Another unforeseen benefit is that your baby is a chick magnet. Now, I have no idea why this is true, but it's been my experience that there's nothing more irresistible to a woman than a man who's alone in public with a baby.

I know this sounds sexist and stereotypical, but it's a phenomenon that I've not only experienced, I've also witnessed it time and again. I don't know if it's because a man taking care of a baby is sexy, or if it's just that a guy with a baby probably isn't a jerk. More likely, it's the attractiveness of the baby itself, and the fact that it's with a man somehow makes it more approachable. I've long suspected that new mothers give off some sort of pheromone detectable only by other women that just screams 'STAY AWAY FROM MY BABY!"

But, no matter the reason, women seem to flock to babies who are accompanied only by men. I recently witnessed this at a department store, where there was a man alone with twin infants. In this case, the mother had accompanied them, but she was away for a time in the ladies room. The man was soon surrounded by an all-female throng who were cooing over the babies and inundating him with questions. When the mother returned, she stood off to the side and surveyed the scene quietly. When the women realized the mother had returned, they scattered.

But my favorite benefit is that you can mold your baby's face into whatever hilarious expression you want and there's nothing they can do about it. You can make it smile. You can make it frown. You can push its nose up and make it look like a baby pig.

Women are generally horrified by this, but I find it very cathartic after changing 100 diapers. "Ha! You may have forced me into the indignity of wiping your butt a million times, but you can't stop me from making your face look ridiculous."

There is, of course, a small window of opportunity for you to use your children's faces to make funny expressions. My children are older and no longer allow me to do this.

14. YOUR CHILD WILL EMBARRASS YOU

One day, when my daughter was about 2 years old, her mother was toweling her off after a bath. Standing there naked, and having nothing better to do at the moment, she used it as an opportunity to explore her backside, when she suddenly started screaming.

It seems that she had never up to this point come across her butt crack. Either she thought it was a deformity or an injury. In any case, she decided it didn't belong there and launched into a minor panic.

Her mother took charge of the situation by saying, "Relax. It's just the crack in your butt. Everybody has one. Jesus put it there."

This revelation seemed to placate her, and she suddenly got very quiet, as though she was processing this information and storing it for retrieval at a later date.

Unfortunately, that later date turned out to be Sunday in church.

As you can imagine, they tend to invoke the name of Jesus a lot at church. I could actually hear my daughter thinking, "Hmmm ... Jesus. Where have I heard that name before?"

So she sat in silence searching her brain bank. And when I say "silence," I mean really, really silent. It was one of those moments in a church service where you can hear a pin drop. It was during this same moment that the recollection came upon her like a thunderclap.

In the midst of this solemn moment, she announced loudly to the congregation at large that "Jesus put the crack in my butt!"

Now, there's nothing you can do to prepare for such a moment. And there's also nothing you can do once the moment happens. Think about it. Do you say anything? And if so, what?

"I apologize for my daughter's blasphemy."

Or

"She's just starting to learn the basics of religious doctrine."

Or

"Sorry for her outburst. We'll leave now and make plans to move to another town."

No, what you will do in this situation is give your child a gentle "Shhh!" and then pretend that nothing happened. For there is nothing you can do.

Actually, that's not true. There is one thing — payback.

You can store up all these incidents like a treasure and return the embarrassment in kind by relating these stories to your children when they are adults — preferably in front of a microphone at their wedding.

Or, you know, in a published book.

And your child may be the warmest, sweetest, most loving creature that ever inhabited the globe — the kind of child who utters nothing but joyous platitudes, every one of which is a treasure from heaven.

It doesn't matter. They will choose a quiet crowded place to suddenly demonstrate such latent traits as racial insensitivity, an intolerance of fat people, inappropriate comments about the handicapped, and (my favorite) gender confusion.

At my wedding, my very young nephew was seated at a table with an older, short-haired woman who was fawning all over him. He was just staring at her and soaking it all in for some time when he turned to his father and asked (loudly, of course) "Is that a dude?"

In the words of the great Mark Twain, "Let us draw the curtain of charity over the rest of the scene."

15. PRIVATE PARTS

One day when my son was first learning how to dress himself but was still having a little trouble, we were hosting a party in our home. It was getting late, but the house was still crowded. So I told my son it was time to get his pajamas on.

We went up to his room where he told me he needed privacy to get changed. He then closed the door behind him, while I delightedly returned to our guests.

The reason I was delighted is that this was another wonderful moment in childhood development. First, it was something else he could do on his own without my help. More importantly, he understood the concept of privacy. This is important for a parent, because you always worry about how you're going to handle those awkward little moments when you have to explain to your children that private parts are private.

My joy, however, was short lived when about two minutes later he was standing completely naked in the middle of a room full of people to tell me he was having difficulty with his shirt, which was inside-out.

This was only the first of many times where he would alternate between demanding privacy and walking around naked. Hopefully, he will have outgrown the habit by the time he goes away to college.

Privacy is a harder concept to teach than you might think, because for some reason children love to run around naked. Granted, it's cute and funny and innocent; still there are certain times when it's less than desirable for them to do this.

Part of explaining all this to them is teaching them about their anatomy. I suggest you do this on a day when you don't have any plans to go anywhere or entertain visitors. You see, when little kids learn a new word, they like to test it. They swish it around in their mouths the way you would sample a new wine.

This is the only explanation I have for the number of times I've heard little girls open conversations with total strangers at the grocery store by saying, "I have a vagina!"

So you can see where it might be better to have your daughter say this sentence over and over in the quiet solace of her own home than, say, in the receiving line at Grandpa's funeral.

But it doesn't end there. Another fun part of explaining the concept of privacy is teaching little boys not to grab themselves in public.

Now, when a little boy is playing, or engaging in some other fun activity, the very last thing he wants to do is stop to go to the bathroom. He could be 10 seconds away from virtual bladder explosion and still refuse to tear himself away from his train set.

Fortunately, there is a warning sign long before it comes to that — the pee-pee dance. I would call it a cross between an Irish jig and a baseball player adjusting his protective cup. When you witness this move, your best bet is taking the little boy quickly to the nearest bathroom. Don't ask, "Do you have to go to the bathroom?" He will say "no" while in the very process of grabbing his crotch and jumping frantically from one leg to the other.

He'll emerge from the bathroom happier, more relaxed and about a couple of quarts lighter; but he'll still refuse to admit he had to go.

But learning privacy is a long, drawn-out process. In fact, if you're trying to think of things to put on your baby shower registry, I strongly recommend a lock for your bedroom door. As soon as a child has mastered the doorknob, he will freely open any door without the slightest consideration of what may be happening on other side of it.

Sure, you can teach them about knocking, but it won't make a difference if they're excited about something and want to tell you. Excitement trumps manners. It won't matter if you're changing, peeing, or engaging in any other activity for which you do not want an audience.

Come to think of it, you may want to make that lock a priority.

16. THE ONLY THING WE HAVE TO FEAR

One of the most heart-wrenching things you deal with as a parent is fear. I don't mean your own (See: You will Lose Your Child). I mean when your baby or toddler experiences real terror.

It's not the kind of fear that grown-ups feel. And it's certainly not the same things grown-ups are afraid of: public speaking, health issues, the IRS.

No, your child will be afraid of mundane, everyday things that are not the least bit scary to you but will nonetheless throw your child into a state of abject terror.

It could be any old thing. Each child is different.

Like a predator fixed on its prey, he bounded for our table
— undoubtedly with the nefarious purpose of giving her a
coloring book.

For my sister, it was a television commercial. Something about the haunting melody of "I Wish I Were an Oscar Mayer Wiener" just threw her synapses into chaos and she would begin crying.

For my daughter, it was clowns.

Now, I have nothing but the greatest respect for the timeless art of clowning. It's ancient, it's honorable, it's even Shakespearian.

But they also happen to be garish, grotesque and scare the living crap out of a certain segment of the population.

It all started one night at a local restaurant. My daughter, who was about 2 at the time, was so excited about her usual fare of macaroni and cheese. This particular evening, as we found out at the restaurant, was Family Fun Night. It included games, prizes, arts and crafts — that sort of thing.

Great, I thought, something to keep her occupied, and maybe she can even socialize with other little children. It was a nice gimmick to pull families in on one of the slow nights of the week.

It was also run by a particularly flamboyant clown.

At first, we were OK. We were on one side of the restaurant and the clown was on the other. To be sure, my daughter kept a wary eye on him, but she was protected by the safety of distance. So she cautiously dined on her macaroni and cheese while never letting him out of her sight.

Then he spotted her.

Like a predator fixed on its prey, he bounded for our table — undoubtedly with the nefarious purpose of giving her a coloring book.

In her mind, however, he was coming to eat her.

She broke into a fit of hysterical screaming that sent the poor painted man fleeing in terror. We also fled. A lengthy session of hugging and about 15 minutes of screaming in my car seemed to be all the therapy she needed to get over this traumatic experience.

OK, I thought, so she's afraid of clowns. That should be easy enough to deal with. I'll just avoid those places clowns tend to frequent — circuses, carnivals, those tiny little cars — and we'll be fine. What I didn't take into consideration is the clown that would seek her out in the safest place in the world — Grandma's house.

It was just a couple of weeks after the restaurant incident, and all was forgotten — by her anyway. I was experiencing post traumatic clown disorder.

Grandma and Grandpa were watching her while I ran a few errands. It was a beautiful spring day, so they decided to sit out on the front steps with her to wait for me.

She was toddling around the yard, sniffing the crocuses and whatnot, when a car pulled up. Normally, people get excited when a celebrity saunters up their front walk. But not this time.

It seems Ronald McDonald was lost and was looking for directions.

Now I don't know where he was heading — a birthday party, a fundraiser, maybe just looking for his way back to McDonaldland. Back then there was no such thing as a McGPS. But it's doubtful he could hear Grandpa's directions over the strident screaming of my traumatized daughter. He finally gave up, decided to seek directions elsewhere, and he and my daughter parted — enemies.

By the time I got there, she was just rocking back and forth muttering, "Go away, clown."

So the point is, as much as you may want to protect your children from the horrors of the world — real or imagined — you can't. So just practice your comforting skills and let them cry when they need to. There's nothing wrong with it.

On a bright note, I learned one very interesting fact that day: Apparently Ronald McDonald drives a beat-up Pinto.

17. INJURING YOUR CHILD

Oh, prepare yourself for the injuries! This is another thing that is unavoidable, regardless of the safety measures you may employ. Injuries are as much a part of childhood as diapers and naptime.

When my daughter was about 6 months old, I accidentally clocked her in the head with a rather large book. Ironically, it was a copy of *What to Expect the First Year*. That book was written for parents. If it had been written for babies, it would probably tell them to expect your father to hit you in the head with a large book.

I understand this is no great revelation to you. Everybody knows that booboos happen. That's why we keep first-aid kits handy. Nevertheless, it's important to psychologically prepare yourself so you don't become completely unglued when the moment arrives.

For me, it was when my son had just begun walking. We were visiting Grandpa and were out on the patio when the boy decided to show off his mad walking skills. He toddled around grasping patio furniture rather adroitly, when he suddenly collapsed under his own weight, cutting his lip on the one table on the patio that wasn't made out of wicker. This was doubly difficult, because not only was he upset, but Grandpa was even more upset — probably because of the copious amounts of blood pouring from his grandson's open wound.

I rushed him inside to the bathroom to treat his injury, when I made a fascinating discovery: my son had never seen blood before.

We were standing in front of a large mirror when he caught the reflection of his blood-soaked face. And he thought it was the funniest thing he had ever seen.

Not only did it become very difficult to clean him up, there is something more than a little creepy and disquieting about a toddler covered with blood and laughing maniacally.

While that incident had a happy if not bizarre ending, it doesn't always turn out that way. Sooner or later, you'll find yourself in the emergency room.

It was right around the same time as the blood laughter incident. Being a little more cautious now with watching him as he walked, I was holding his hands up over his head so he wouldn't come crashing down on anything.

Big mistake.

He did fall, but this time, rather than hitting anything, he began cradling his arm and screaming. It was a nice, steady scream — the kind that indicates to the parent that all is not well. So I brought him to the emergency room.

Let me state this as straightforward as possible: when you bring your child to the emergency room for an injury, they will assume you are a criminal — that you torture your children for fun.

Don't be upset about this. It's their job. You see, they have to convince themselves that your child is not being beaten by you, so they'll ask you all sorts of questions hinting at the fact that they think you're a child beater. They think they're being subtle. But in reality, they're about as subtle as the guy in the next room who's looking to score some oxycontin.

They ask questions like, "So, how did this happen?" "Yes, but how *exactly* did this happen?" "Can you describe everything in detail?"

And you won't be asked this string of awkward questions just once. Oh no. The doctor will ask you, the nurse will ask you, the X-ray tech will ask you. The guy who figures out your bill will ask you, and the guy mopping the floor will ask you.

In my case, after enduring this interrogation, the doctor came in, grabbed my sons arm and popped it. Then the screaming stopped. It seems he had something called nursemaid's elbow or babysitter's elbow. It should be called "parent's elbow" because I'm certain this is something that happens mostly on the parents' watch.

It's simply a dislocation of the elbow joint that can occur because the little one's joints and ligaments are still growing. The doctor was even good enough to show me how to pop it back into place, just in case it happened again.

I'm proud to report that I was careful enough in the future that it never happened again. By about the age of 3, your child's ligaments will be strong enough where this is no longer a concern.

And that's good, because around that time you can start moving on to the bigger concerns of cuts, black eyes and broken bones.

The broken bone came when the boy had just turned 6. This was the worst one of all. He was in a lot of pain, there was a lot of blood, and we were in a public place. Worst of all, my wife was there. She was not psychologically prepared.

We were at a playground and the boy was climbing the ladder to the slide. His back was to us, so I didn't get to see it all, but he fell on his hands. At first he seemed OK. I even yelled, "Walk it off!"

I felt like a jerk when he turned around screaming — blood pouring from his hand. To this day, I don't know how he did it. But when he fell, he not only broke his thumb, he ripped the thumbnail clear off.

I grabbed him and rushed him to the car while the playground mothers were all shouting various pieces of advice at me. But I knew there was only one place to go: the E/R. I also knew I was in for another awkward interrogation. But such is life.

My wife's state of mind was one I would call restrained hysteria. She was also more than a little nauseated. All the way to the hospital, I just prayed she wasn't about to reupholster my car seats.

Fortunately, she rallied admirably. She never let the boy know she was upset or worried. She talked to him and kept his spirits up while I checked in and answered the awkward questions.

She also made up a new family rule: when you go to the emergency room, you get to have ice cream for dinner.

My son was cool with that.

18. YOU WILL LOSE YOUR CHILD

At some point you will misplace your child.

Now, I know what you're thinking; "That won't happen to me. I'm going to be a responsible and attentive parent."

You're deluding yourself. You will lose your child. No matter how alert you are, no matter how responsible you may be, even if you have one of those dog leashes that the overzealous parents use to tether their offspring, you will lose your child.

Whether it's a five-second scare because they've crawled under a garment rack at a clothing store, or during rush hour in midtown Manhattan, it is an inevitability.

And understand this is no reflection on you as a person or your parenting skills. It even happened to Jesus. His own practically perfect parents lost him on their annual trip to the big city. ("I thought he was with you." "No, I thought he was with you!")

It happened to me twice with my son.

The first time was in Target when he was about 2 or 3. He and I were looking at the toys. My attention was riveted on some particularly interesting board games, when I noticed the boy was nowhere to be found. I ran up and down aisles, yelling his name — all to no avail.

It turns out that he simply walked around an end-cap to look at more toys when he was immediately accosted by a woman who was horrified to see a little boy untethered.

The whole thing could have ended then and there except for the question she chose to ask: "Where is your mommy?" to which he shrugged and said, "I don't know."

Of course he didn't know, he hadn't seen her all day.

If she had instead asked, "Where is your mommy or daddy?" he would have said, "Oh, Daddy is over there looking at toys."

But the woman assumed that a child couldn't be anywhere but in the company of his female parent, so she took it upon herself to bring him to the customer service desk, where the boy cheerily provided them with his name and other vital statistics.

The lady at the desk knew just what to do, and her voice boomed over the loudspeaker, saying, "Mrs. Trafford, please report to the front desk."

Et tu, customer service representative?

When I came running, I found the boy quietly and patiently munching on something. "Look, Daddy," he said. "They bought me popcorn."

The second time was when he was 6 and it was a little more harrowing. It was in a corn maze that covered about five acres. And it was getting dark. And my wife was with us.

Now I know what you're thinking: What kind of an idiot would let a 6-year-old boy run off by himself in a corn maze?

This kind of idiot, that's who.

But let me explain. The corn maze comes with a map so you can find your way through fairly easily. But this one had a gimmick: at various places hidden through the maze there were different shaped hole punches. If you punched your ticket with all of them you could win a prize.

At one corner of the maze, it was obvious looking at the map that the path just circled back to where we were. But we still had to check it out, because one of the hole punches might be there. Being particularly lazy that day, I told my son to run around the circle and meet me back to let me know if he saw a hole punch.

He followed my instructions perfectly.

Well, almost.

You see, along this maze, near the outside were several "emergency exits" so people could leave the maze and walk back if they were, tired, ill, or just sick of the maze. They were all clearly marked.

Except one.

That's right, the boy ran out the exit outside the maze, then back into the maze through another exit. After a while, when I realized he should have been back by now, I went looking for him and realized what happened. By that time he was somewhere deep in the bowels of the maze.

I was beside myself.

My wife was hysterical.

I told her to stay put and I would run to the start of the maze. At the entrance, they had a high wooden platform that overlooked the whole cornfield. Unfortunately, it wasn't high enough. I could see the top of the cornstalks, but that's it.

As I descended the stairs, I was wondering what the poor boy must be experiencing. He was lost and alone. It was getting darker by the minute. He must be terrified.

I was just about ready to call in the cavalry when he came cheerfully skipping out of the maze's exit.

Not only did he find his way through it alone and without a map, he had the presence of mind to tag his ticket with the rest of the hole punches along the way.

I saw no need to let the boy know about the incredible trauma I just experienced, so I brought him back to my wife, who hugged him as though she hadn't seen him in 10 years, and blurted out, "Oh my God! I was so scared! I thought you were lost!"

At which time, the boy burst into tears and was inconsolable for the next 15 minutes.

So be prepared when this happens to you, because it will.

Just don't panic.

19. WAITING FOR SOMETHING TO DEVELOP

At some point, your baby or toddler is going to do something absolutely amazing. Maybe he will speak in complete sentences at 6 months old. Maybe she will be able to recite all the presidents at a year old. Maybe he'll be able to re-plumb a boiler at 2.

It doesn't matter what it is, because you will be convinced your little tyke is a genius. You will tell all your friends and relatives. You'll shout it from the parapets (or the modern-day version of that, which is posting it on Facebook).

You will daydream about your child winning the Nobel Prize. Even better, you will daydream about your child being able to bankroll you to a comfortable early retirement. Get all these thoughts out of your head. Your child is probably not a genius. Or maybe he is. It's just that amazing baby feats are not a very good gauge of that.

You hear a lot about child development. It's today's big thing. Parents are naturally excited about seeing their child grow and develop. They even do it in utero. "This week your baby is the size of an olive. He has webbed fingers and his heart is beating."

The next week it'll be the size of a cumquat. (I don't know why food is the standard unit of fetus measurement, but then I'm not a medical professional). The next week he'll be the size of a fig, ballroom dancing and doing his own taxes.

The problem with all of this is that when the child doesn't fall into the accepted pattern of development as set down in the textbooks, parents freak out. Either they think there is something very wrong or they think their child is an unbelievable prodigy. Most of the time, neither is true. Of course, there are developmental alarm bells you should keep in mind.

I'm just saying don't measure your kid against an arbitrary latitude of growth and longitude of development or you're likely to give yourself a stroke. Just let your kid grow at his or her own rate.

Think back to the first time you started shaving. Were you the same exact age as every other boy in your class? Ask your wife if every girl in her class got her period at the same age. My guess is she'll tell you they ranged in age from 9 to 14, even though 12 was the average. Just avoid using the word "normal" because there's no such thing.

I'm six-foot-one. I know lots of men who are five-foot-seven, and a few who are six-foot-four. Which is normal? The answer, of course, is that nothing is. Well, the same goes for rates of development. I don't mean to take that to the extreme or anything. If your daughter is 15 and hasn't gotten her period, it's probably time to call the doctor.

But if your kindergartner can barely manage a stick figure when some of his classmates are already showing knowledge of lighting and perspective, you probably don't have to take him in for testing.

This seems as good a place as any to mention this: if you have a kid who's left handed and neither you nor your wife is, cut him some slack. My son, who just loves cutting up paper, had some serious trouble staying in the lines when using scissors. In fact, he was so bad at it that I was considering having him tested. Then it finally dawned on me: he's a lefty.

There are all sorts of things you have to keep in mind when you have a left-handed kid. Throwing is different. It can be difficult to track down a baseball glove. And I can't even imagine how weird it must be for him to shake hands. But the scissors thing caught me off-guard. You see, scissors are asymmetrical. So if you're trying to cut paper with your left hand, it's a Herculean task. For all you righties out there, try it if you don't believe me. Anyway, I tracked down some left-handed scissors for him and everything is cool now. I suggest you do the same if you have a little southpaw.

20. HOARDING THE TREASURES OF CHILDHOOD

The first time your child comes home from nursery school or kindergarten or whatever, you will be presented by his or her first dabbling in art. It will be an indistinguishable blotch of goopy color on construction paper.

You will treat this like it's the frickin' Mona Lisa.

You have to. For one thing, you will be pretty excited. For another, your child will be delighted. Most importantly, you want to build up your child's self-esteem. Apparently the best way to do this is by acting like this is the greatest moment in art history since Michelangelo first picked up a chisel.

"I love it! It's beautiful! We'll have to find a special place for this one!"

You will display this piece of work. You will then put it away in a safe place to be treasured always.

You will also be setting the excited reaction bar pretty high for all other work your child does.

Of course, you can't keep everything. But there is absolutely no way of explaining this to a child. By the first grade, they're coming home every week with enough papers to make a telephone directory.

(For those of you not old enough, a telephone directory was a large book with everybody's phone number in it. Realizing how dated the metaphor is, I thought about changing it to a Sears catalog, but abandoned it for the same reason. Then I thought about Webster's dictionary. Then I finally just gave up.)

And it doesn't end with school work. Around this same time, your child will be consumed with the wonders of making stuff with paper — writing, drawing, gluing, cutting and taping. There is no way to track down the thousands of little paper triangles that will go fluttering to the floor during this phase.

Your home will be strewn with so much paper, it'll look like Times Square after a ticker tape parade.

(For those of you not old enough, ticker tape was this thin paper from machines that told you how the stock market was doing. Sigh. This is depressing me.)

Anyway, as I said, you can't keep it all. So you have to discard some of it. But when you do, your child may come looking for whatever he gave to you.

The best way to avoid this is to keep these little treasures for a certain amount of time (maybe a week). If it hasn't been mentioned, then it's probably a safe bet that the little tyke has forgotten about it, and it may now be discarded.

Just make sure — and I speak from experience — that your child does not find these discarded treasures.

My son is in the first grade, and every Friday, he comes home with a folder full of the schoolwork he's done that week. I swear to God, he pushes more paper than the average civil servant.

I go through all of it to see how he's doing in school. Then I fold it up neatly and put it in the recycling bin.

This system worked fine for several weeks — until the day he found the discarded school work.

The following is what he said to me, verbatim, with tears in his eyes.

"I was shocked — *shocked* — to find my schoolwork in the trash. I worked really, really hard on that, and you just threw it all away."

Granted, this was not my proudest parenting moment. But it wasn't my worst, either.

When my wife came home and I related the story to her, she said, "You can't throw it away so that he'll find it, you have to be stealthy."

Thanks, honey. There's nothing more helpful than somebody else's hindsight.

It took a little while to console him, but we sat down at the negotiating table and came to an agreement whereby I would go through all the weekly work with him and let him decide what to keep and what to toss.

When next Friday came, he decided that every last scrap of paper should be kept. Not having the funds to rent a storage unit just for his schoolwork, it looks like I'm going to have to go back to discarding most of it. But don't worry; I shall do so as surreptitiously as possible.

I do keep a box of much of his stuff. And I still have the very first thing he ever made in preschool. When he's an adult, I plan to frame it and give it to him. Maybe that will make up for my indiscretion with the recycling bin.

21. MAKE WAY FOR BIRTHDAYS

I remember my eighth birthday.

I don't remember it because anything wonderful happened, or because I got the best birthday present, or I had a kickass party.

It started out pretty well for no other reason than it was a Saturday, so I had no school. It was also 1980, so we had already begun to wake from the aesthetic nightmare of the 1970s.

But what made it so memorable was that in the morning I went out with my father. I forget the reason. Probably so he could buy a newspaper. Remember, this was back in the era when people bought newspapers. While we were in the pharmacy where he used to purchase his news, I spotted a squirt gun. I wanted it.

Now, whenever I saw something I wanted in a store, I almost never asked my father for it, knowing that the answer would invariably be no. But today was different. Maybe because it was such a beautiful spring day, maybe because it was my birthday, maybe it was because my father had just won $2 on a scratch ticket, I don't know. What I do know is that I decided to boldly ask him to purchase the squirt gun for me.

To my delight and astonishment, he said yes, and shelled out the 35 cents for it.

It was a small see-through green plastic pistol, and it held little more than an ounce of water. But I thought it was the greatest thing in the world. I spent the rest of that balmy spring day alternately refilling it at the outside faucet and shooting the hosta plants that lined the front walk.

I remember nothing else of that day. I assume I opened birthday presents. Don't know what they were. I assume some relatives came over and we had some cake. Don't remember anything about it — or any other birthday before or since.

All I remember is that squirt gun.

There's a reason for that. You see, I was an 8-year-old boy. And like all 8-year-old boys, it didn't take much to make me happy.

Of course, that was then. This is now.

My guess is that little boys and girls are probably still pretty easy to please. But it doesn't matter. Because you're going to get sucked into the birthday party phenomenon.

Remember all that crap — cliques, social awkwardness, self-esteem issues, one-ups-manship — you left behind in high school? You only thought you said goodbye to those things forever. Well, they're back in the form of kids' birthday parties.

I'm not sure why, but there is tremendous pressure among parents these days to show the world what wonderful moms or dads they are. I've seen mothers who have created candy-coated confections for their kids' classrooms that would rival the world's best bakeries.

Everyone tries to impress and outdo each other by baking the most impressive cookies at the bake sale, or buying their kids the best backpack, or of course, throwing the best birthday party.

I've been to a number of these now, and the impressiveness of them seems to be directly proportional to a community's affluence. I've seen them in bowling alleys, bouncy houses, indoor trampoline parks, even tae kwon do studios. I've never seen one at somebody's home.

There's something else you should know. It's now the custom to invite every last one of your kid's classmates to these birthday parties. Schools now will happily distribute invitations, but they have to be for every kid in the class, so there won't be any situations like Charlie Brown being the only kid not to get one. Of course, you can always send out the invitations outside of school, but it won't do you any good. The kids who are invited will talk about it to the kids who aren't invited and it'll turn into this big thing.

Also, your child will be disappointed and probably cry. Why? Because apparently, they discourage kids from opening birthday presents at these things. There's only a limited amount of time you get at an indoor trampoline park. There's just enough time to bounce around and swallow a piece of cake. Then it's like a jailbreak out of there. The presents are opened at home. I don't know if this is the policy of the establishment. Maybe they don't want to deal with wrapping paper. Or maybe it's the policy of the parents. They don't want to deal with any embarrassment from the kid not liking a present, duplication, etc. Anyway, it sucks a lot of the joy right out of the occasion.

I don't know how much money parents shell out for these things. I don't know because I've never hosted one. Realizing it may make me a social pariah in the parenting world, I nonetheless opted for something a little more low-key in celebrating my kids' birthdays.

What you decide is up to you. It probably depends on how susceptible you are to peer pressure. I will tell you only this. If you do have it at one of the best kids' party venues in your community, I guarantee that you will spend a lot of time standing around talking to fathers who will say stuff like "We never did this sort of thing when I was a kid."

On the other hand, it will give you good experience for when it comes time to plan your kid's wedding. And it will make you used to shelling out bucketloads of money for your child's latest social event.

I sometimes wish I had experienced this sort of thing in my youth. But then I wonder if I would remember it as well as I do that 35-cent squirt gun.

Man, I've got to get myself one of those.

I bet the price has gone up, though.

22. THE TALK

One hot summer's day, when the boy was about 5 years old, we were both busy cleaning out the shed. The place was a mess and needed straightening out in the worst way. There hadn't been much conversation between us, as we were both pretty occupied in our respective chores (that's right, I put my 5-year-old son to work; but in my defense, it doesn't nearly equal what I pay him in terms of room and board. But I digress.)

Anyway, I have no idea what put this idea into his head — I would have loved to follow his train of thought — but he suddenly asked me, "Daddy, do all women get pregnant?"

Now, if you're not ready for it, that's the sort of question that can make you freeze up and panic. What should I say? How much should I say? Is my answer just going to lead to more questions?

It's always been my policy not to lie to my children — for the most part. But then there's this whole prevarication about Santa Claus I've been perpetuating for years, so sometimes it's a gray area.

I could always say, "I don't know," or "Ask your mother." But I didn't want to wimp out either. So I said this: "No, not all women. You have to be just the right age. Young girls can't be pregnant. And old women can't be pregnant. But it can only happen to women. Men can't get pregnant. You know that right?"

"Yeah, I know that," he said with a nod.

The answer must have satisfied him, because there were no follow-up questions. Of course, I realize I may have misled him just a little bit. I made it sound like pregnancy is something that just happens, like facial hair just happens to a man.

To be perfectly honest, I have no idea what I would have said if he had sprung any more questions on me. I was expecting "How does the baby come out?" or the more disquieting "How does the baby get in?"

Fortunately, he was with his mother when he broached the topic of how the baby comes out. It seems she had a problem with his belief that women "just poop the baby out" so she gave him a quick lesson on female anatomy. Again, he was satisfied.

I don't know why we get so uncomfortable when discussing sex with our kids. I guess we put such a moral and religious taint on it that we can't imagine the sexual act as being something our innocent little children would ever engage in — even in adulthood. And to be fair, from their point of view, the first thing they'll picture in their little minds is their parents performing said act, which to them would seem the most disgusting thing in the world.

When the younger of my two sisters asked our mother where babies come from, she was ordered to go to her bedroom. My mother told her she would be in to tell her all about it. About half an hour or so later, after my mother had summoned up the courage, she went in and spilled it all. My sister listened attentively, then blurted out, "Gross! You had to do that three times?"

But as uncomfortable as that talk is, it's as necessary as teaching your kids to read — or rather it's as necessary as teaching your kids not to touch a hot stove. That way you can avoid a whole lot of unpleasantness later on, such as bad reputations, bad decisions, STDs, or worst of all, grandchildren.

In my own case, I went to Catholic school. Always believing that knowledge is the best policy, they told us all about sex explicitly. And to make sure it was done morally, ethically and above board, the parish priest came in to give the talk. There was even a slideshow with cross-sections of penises and uteruses to make sure we grasped everything. The fact that he had to stop continually because many of the slides were in upside-down probably just caused a lot of confusion among those young minds, but that's another story for another time. Suffice to say, if you think talking to your parents about sex is uncomfortable, try listening to a parish priest use words like "engorged" and "penetrated." I would rather have heard all about it from my grandparents.

You'll have to decide how much you want to get into specifics, depending on your kid's age and maturity level. When it comes to girls, it's probably best to let a women handle telling them about what's going to happen to their bodies. Just make sure the women in your life don't wait too long. Whatever age they think it's going to happen, make it two years younger, just to be on the safe side. You don't want any girls to be caught unawares. That could have terrible repercussions.

Just watch the movie "Carrie."

23. DISCIPLINE

When I was a kid, there was nothing more exciting than waking up on Christmas morning. For me and my sisters, it involved a ritual. We would wake up, get dressed, go to church at 7 a.m., come home, cook breakfast, eat breakfast, wash the dishes and put them away. Then — and only then — did my father allow us to open our presents.

It's what I grew up with, so it never occurred to me at the time that it was anything other than the Christmas morning norm. When I tell people about this today, they look at me like my father was a lunatic. He wasn't. He was just determined to teach and enforce discipline. Just because it was

Christmas, that was no reason to let things devolve into chaos and anarchy. He was so obsessed with maintaining that discipline, that he actually set up booby traps to catch my sisters in the act of trying to peek into the living room.

It was separated from the rest of the house by a door into the kitchen. So on Christmas Eve, my father would shut it, and then rest a plate on the floor standing up against the living room side of the door. Then he would leave the house through one door and come back in through another. That way, if any of us kids tried to open the door to peek, it would cause the plate to come crashing down, thus alarming him to our transgression.

OK, maybe he was a little bit of a lunatic.

The point is that it made me extremely disciplined. Today, I am the most patient person I know. It also made me a big believer in teaching kids what is expected of them, though my wife made it abundantly clear that we were not going to adopt my father's Christmas traditions. In fact, she introduced me to her family's tradition of opening one gift on

Christmas Eve — an indulgence that would undoubtedly have given my old man a heart attack.

While I am by no means the stickler he was (in today's culture that would be tantamount to cruelty), I do believe in teaching children a modicum of discipline early on. This will keep them from riding roughshod over you.

Sometime over the past 25 years, it became in vogue to give misbehaving children a "timeout." I have witnessed several parents do this. When little Johnny is misbehaving, they make him sit down and be quiet for a predetermined amount of time, like a tiny little hockey player in a penalty box. I have never seen this successfully curb the child's tendency toward whatever delinquency merited the timeout in the first place.

My strategy is a little different, but I'm sure it would horrify many. No, it doesn't involve physical or psychological abuse. But it does involve an investment of time. And that's what scares most parents. I think one of the reasons the "timeout" was so attractive to parents is that it allowed them to keep on doing whatever it was they were doing while the kid just sat, fumed and fidgeted. Whenever one of my kids misbehaved, I immediately removed them from wherever we happened to be, and took them to a quiet room. And we talked about it. And we talked about it. And we talked about it some more.

OK, so it was kind of like a timeout; the difference is that I was taking the timeout right along with them. They say you can't reason with children, and maybe that's true. But I will say this: after a few times of doing this, the need for them became fewer and fewer. And by the age of 3, the kids didn't need these talks anymore.

People tend to bristle at the word "discipline." I think maybe they find it synonymous with "punishment." Really, discipline just means self-control. And just as you teach a child to control his, legs, bladder and fine motor skills, you must also teach him to control his temper and behavior.

It almost seems like the more time parents invest in their children today, the less time they seem to spend with their child one on one. Oh, there's a lot of time spent planning, driving, baking, setting up, taking down, etc. The list goes on and on. But all these activities require a sacrifice. And I fear that for many parents, that sacrifice is one-on-one time with their kids.

Don't get me wrong. I've been criticized a lot. Some have told me that I expect too much from my kids. But I find it interesting that they always tell me this only after observing how well-behaved the kids are.

Of course, every kid is different. And there are some real behavioral disorders out there. When I hear a kid screaming in the grocery store and some adult makes a rude comment about it, I can't help thinking that we have no idea what that parent or child is going through. Maybe the child is autistic and he or she just encountered a sight, sound or smell that was unfamiliar and it was just too much for the little tyke. It's hard, but I always try to be understanding.

But behavioral disorders aside, I see no reason why children can't be taught self-control, empathy and respect for others. It takes time, but it's not that hard.

Maybe putting a plate up against the door once in a while isn't such a bad idea.

24. WILL YOU GO OUT WITH ME?

One of the nice things — if not the nicest thing — about being married is that you don't have to date anymore. You don't have to worry about where to meet girls, where to take them, awkward conversation or the even more awkward end of the date.

Actually, scratch that. That's a big fat lie. You'll be going through that all over again. It's called the playdate. You see, back when I was a kid, we didn't have playdates. The parents of children in my generation couldn't be bothered with such things — more evidence of the wisdom of our parents. No, back then we were encouraged to go outside and make sure we were in by the time the street lights came on.

But apparently today, that would be roughly the equivalent of giving your kids some matches and a bottle of whiskey and telling them to leave you alone for the rest of the day.

So, we have playdates. That way we can make sure our little ones are socializing in a healthy, controlled environment. And we parents can be right there to step in and squash any incidents that may arise.

When my son was about 3 years old, I heard a lot of criticism from people who told me I wasn't doing enough to nurture his social instinct. After all, the last thing I wanted on my hands was for my son to be the only cigarette-smoking, leather jacket-wearing anti-hero in kindergarten. So it was imperative that I work on his socialization skills with kids his own age. Again, this was in the early days of Facebook, and the newsfeed was filled with mothers prattling on about their kids' latest playdate. "Great!" I thought. "I'll just get in on a little bit of that."

The first person I contacted was a woman I knew with a little girl about my son's age. I sent her a Facebook message inviting her and her daughter to a playdate. She responded in the negative while making more than a subtle hint that she thought I was hitting on her. That was the first and last time I ever attempted to make a playdate. From then on, I refused. I didn't care how much criticism they piled on me. I didn't care if my son grew up to be a sociopath. I wasn't going through that again.

So, I always let the women in my life handle that. And I'm glad I did — because just sitting back and watching the drama unfold is better than reality television.

Your strong, mature, professional wife will suddenly regress to an awkward high school girl before your very eyes. The same woman who blazed a career path with confidence and intelligence will be wringing her hands worrying about whether the other mothers like her.

First, there's the initial contact. Usually your child will develop certain friendships in the early days of kindergarten, and then talk about inviting so-and-so over. In my son's school, they hand out an email list of all the parents at the beginning of the year, so contacting these parents is never a problem.

Then there's the first email. Will they say yes? Will they say no? She can't handle that kind of rejection. What if they don't respond at all?

Then, when the big day is finally set up, she'll be nervous about how she looks, how the house looks, what to talk about with the other mother. It will almost be like getting a glimpse of what she was probably like when she first started dating you. Only it will be more intense, because women always try a lot harder to impress other women than they do men. It's a fact. Women acknowledge this fact. They hate this about themselves, yet they continue to do it.

And the only thing worse than going on that first date is wondering whether or not there will be a second one. Try to shift your wife's attention from hanging around the phone all day or constantly checking her email.

Then your wife's newfound friend may start hanging out more with one of the other mothers. And the jealousy will begin. Why does she like her better than me? What's wrong with me?

Oh yeah, it'll be a barrel of laughs.

But it's all worth it, because apparently your kids will have so much cultural interaction and develop such strong interpersonal skills, they'll be ready for a job with the State Department.

Your wife, however, will develop the haggard look of a person who defuses bombs all day long.

25. THE SPORTING LIFE

I don't have too many fond memories of my days in Little League. That's mostly because I was the worst right fielder in the history of the Superior Bakery Expos. Oh, I loved baseball, and I loved playing. I just wasn't any good at it. I couldn't throw, I couldn't hit, and I couldn't catch. And that's really rough, because when you're a little boy, you tend to be judged by your peers on your ability to do all those things.

I was judged harshly.

In fact, I was a superlative of the team in only one way: my uniform was the cleanest because I never dirtied it up by sliding into a base. It really bothered me that I was no good at any of those things; although, looking back I can't think of a single time in my life when any of those skills would have been useful.

It bothered me even more because my father was such a huge sports fan. The man eats, breathes and sleeps sports. I have little doubt he would sit and watch cricket on TV if there were nothing else available. In fact, he is so intense in his fandom, that he often has to DVR certain games, because if he watched them live he'd probably have a heart attack screaming at ballplayers, even though they're way too far away to hear the acrimonious tones of his criticism.

Anyway, I got a little bit of an understanding of what they were going through all those years ago, watching me stand in the outfield looking for shapes in the clouds: My son wanted to sign up for T-ball.

I wanted to make sure that's what he wanted to do. No soccer? No tae kwon do? No knife-throwing?

Nope. T-ball. So I signed him up, bought him a glove, bat and uniform and let him go to town. First of all, let me say how saintly and patient each and every T-ball coach is.

One time, a batted ball was heading straight for the head of a little boy whose attention had wandered away from the game and was instead transfixed on what must have been a fascinating blade of grass.

Getting a bunch of 4- and 5-year-olds to throw, catch and hit while behaving as a team is like trying to teach a bunch of chimps to sing the Hallelujah Chorus in harmony. It's a thankless and hopeless task, but damn! They never gave up.

One time, a batted ball was heading straight for the head of a little boy whose attention had wandered away from the game and was instead transfixed on what must have been a fascinating blade of grass. There was an audible gasp, since it was obvious that this ball was going to hit the tiny first baseman on the head. But a nearby coach stuck his bare hand in the path of the ball and took one for the team, so to speak, stopping it just inches away from the little boy's head. The coach got a standing ovation. The little first baseman had no idea what had just happened, as his attention was now focused on a completely different blade of grass.

In any given play, the ball would be hit off the tee after several attempts, and then a few seconds later (after much prodding from the coach) you'd hear the pitter patter of tiny little feet making their way for first base. On top of the boy's tiny little shoulders was an enormous helmet that so weighed him down, as he ran it would make his head bob around from side to side like an ocean buoy in a hurricane.

All of this would generally take about a minute, but it didn't really matter, because the kid could easily make it to second base while three or four members of the opposing team were fighting over which one of them got to field the ball.

And there are no outs in T-ball. Every kid gets to bat in every inning. I could watch all day.

But I never resented it. And although my son's favorite part of the game seemed to be playing in the dirt of the infield, I truly enjoyed watching him out there. As for having to sit through all that, I admit that more than once I thought about my parents doing the same thing.

I like to think I'm paying it forward.

26. WEARING IT BETTER

Long before your child makes its first appearance, you're going to learn all about how to diaper it and swaddle it. You'll get so adept at wrapping that blanket around your baby that Harry Houdini couldn't work his way out of it.

What they won't tell you about is dressing your little one in normal people clothes. But that is an adventure unto itself. My best advice is to try to do this while the child is asleep. Dressing a baby who's fully awake is like roping and hog-tying a calf. Babies can sense when you're trying to dress them, and instinctively start to flail their limbs about uncontrollably. You'll get one leg into a pair of pants, then as you're trying to get the other leg to hold still, the first leg will come popping out again.

Socks are also a nuisance, but the worst is by far the shoes. Women love, love baby shoes. And it's hard to blame them, because they're frickin' adorable. There's just one problem with them: no baby anywhere should ever wear them. Sure, they're cute, but your baby is not going to be walking; your baby is going to be flailing. If you're taking your baby out for the day, at some point you will notice one of the shoes has gone missing. Since babies have nothing better to do than sleep, poop and eat, they will spend the rest of their time devising ways to make their baby shoes go astray. When this happens, your wife will probably yell at you. If you were carrying the baby when it happened, then you should have been more careful. If she was carrying the baby when it happened, then you should have been more alert.

A few weeks ago, I witnessed a couple walking out of a department store with an infant. The man was carrying the little boy, and the wife suddenly said, "Where's his shoe? What did you do, lose it?" The man turned and began frantically retracing his steps when an older woman came out the door brandishing the shoe and asking, "Is this yours?"

I just shook my head and thought, "I give them to the end of the day before one of those shoes is gone forever." My wife, who also witnessed this spectacle, just turned to me and asked, "Why do babies even need shoes anyway?" God, I love her. If your wife feels the same way, then you've got it made. If not, then plan on having a collection of single baby shoes without their mates.

When your baby is a newborn, so many people will give you clothes, you'll start to think that you'll never have to buy this kid anything. Then they grow. A lot. So you'll have to go out and buy clothes yourself. If you have a girl, you've got it made. The selection is staggering.

If you have a boy, however, you'll have a choice between professional sports logos and cartoon characters. I'm not even kidding. Most children's departments seem to cater exclusively to little girls.

Really, it must be a 90/10 ratio. And what's worse, every article of clothing they make for little boys has to have writing on it. I don't know if this is some sort of rule enacted by the Department of Commerce, but apparently it's illegal to manufacture little boy clothing that doesn't have some trite phrase like "Little Slugger."

I actually got in the habit of buying shirts for my son anytime I could find one that didn't have words on it just so I could keep him from looking like a little billboard.

The only thing that's nearly as joyful as the day your kid is toilet trained is the day he or she can dress him or herself. As they age into toddlerhood, you'll still be dressing them — and they'll still be flailing — only now they're heavier and stronger.

Sometimes your kid will be fiercely independent, like my daughter, who insisted on dressing herself at a very early age. Other times, they'll be like my son, who if I had let him, would have had me dressing him till he was 21.

I tried appealing to his sense of independence: "Don't you want to dress yourself like a big boy?" Didn't work.

Finally, I told him that if he dressed himself, he could pick out whatever clothes he wanted to wear. This intrigued him. So he cheerfully set about the task of getting himself dressed. It took a little while, but he did it all by himself. Unfortunately, he was wearing bright green pants, a purple striped T-shirt, and a red plaid button-down shirt over it.

I didn't have the heart to tell him he looked like a fashion nightmare, especially since he was strutting around like he had just leapt off the pages of a Jane Austen novel. I was just glad that he finally did it himself, so I was willing to overlook the fact that he was dressed like a developmentally disabled clown.

My wife, on the other hand, had no intention of letting him go out in public like that. I told her she was on her own. I knew asking him to change after he had already spent so much time on his outfit would cause a huge scene. But she calmly and kindly explained to him about how we match our clothes.

He listened with great interest, and then finally acquiesced to her demands.

There's just one final clothing phenomenon you need to know about: the Halloween costume. It's an exciting thing for a kid to get dressed up and go trick-or-treating.

Just one word of advice: don't get the costume too early. You may be tempted to. Sometime around late September, the costume shops start sprouting up. You may think, "I should get one now while there's still such a huge selection."

The problem is your kid does not want to wait until Halloween to wear the costume. Your kid wants to wear the costume right now. So, after a lot of incessant whining, you'll give in. Then he'll want to wear the costume every day. He won't understand why he's not allowed to go school while wearing his costume. It will cause arguing and heartache. By the time Halloween rolls around, the costume will be little more than a pile of lint.

I'm speaking from experience, here. Try to hold off on buying that costume until just before the big day. Either that or be prepared to go grocery shopping with Batman.

27. WHEN PARENTS BECOME GRAND

Being a grandparent is great. At least I assume it is. It will probably be quite a few years before I find out for sure, but every grandparent I know seems to revel in the role.

And it's no wonder; grandparents feel all the love and joy that you feel toward your kids, but they're burdened with none of the responsibility. My father once told me, "The best thing about grandchildren is that at the end of the day, they go home with the parents." He may have said that tongue in cheek, but I know where he's coming from. My parents already did their time with babies and toddlers and (shudder) teenagers. Now they can just enjoy the grandkids in small doses then ship them back to their parents when they're done with them.

One thing you'll have to look out for is when grandparents have a favorite. This happens a lot, and it can always cause a lot of hard feelings — particularly among the parents. The grandchildren, for the most part, are blissfully unaware of this. But it does happen. And I ought to know, because it happened to me.

Now I won't embarrass my own parents here by telling any stories. Instead, I'll reach back into my childhood for a story involving my own grandparents. I do this because my grandparents are all dead now. And dead people can't sue you for libel. I checked.

My grandmother, that is my mother's mother, was one of those grannies afflicted with having a favorite — my oldest sister. And she made no attempt to conceal the fact from anybody. It's probably because my sister was her first grandchild. Yeah, that must be it. I can't really see any other intrinsic quality in her that would have warranted such favoritism. So let's go with that.

Anyway, her bias toward my sister was so intense, that my mother was never allowed to chastise her in my grandmother's presence. Really. A simple word of chiding against my dear sister would make the poor old woman cry. My sister could've made a mess, knocked over a precious heirloom, or shaved the cat. It didn't matter; my mother would have to take her into another room to have words with her — out of earshot of my grandmother.

That's not to say my sister was a bad seed or anything; more a bit of a fussbudget, like Lucy in the Peanuts comic strip. I should probably stop right there, because my sister *is* still alive and therefore has the ability to bring a suit against me. She probably would, too. Little fussbudget.

It's more than a little weird to watch your parents turn into grandparents. Mine are of the generation that didn't smoke or eat lard for breakfast and so managed to make it into their 70s while remaining healthy and active. And I have to tell you, it's so much nicer having my kids get to know them when they still look and act like normal people.

When I was a kid, all old people looked like wrinkled turtles without the shells. They wore shawls, they smelled funny and they constantly talked about how they were ready for death.

Today's old people are alive and interesting and are actually fun to be around, even if they do know absolutely nothing about pop culture. In fact, if your parents are still spry enough, maybe you can even talk them into some overnighters with the grandkids. After all, it will help keep them young. And that way you and your wife can have some grown-up time, which will keep you from aging too quickly and losing the will to live.

Because just as it's weird to see your parents turn into grandparents, it's nothing compared to seeing yourself turn into them. And it will happen just as sure as the sun will rise tomorrow. And it won't be a gradual thing, either. One day you will open your mouth to talk to your child and your father's voice will come out.

Not too long ago, my son came home from school and threw his coat down on the couch. Before I knew what I was doing, I heard myself saying, "Just a minute, young man! Does that coat belong there?"

Hardly can I express the emotions which seized me as the boy begrudgingly crept back to his coat and went to hang it up in the closet. Because that little boy was me 35 years ago.

And it didn't end there. I found myself uttering phrases like, "These cabinet doors were designed to be closed" or "Don't throw those jeans in the hamper, you only wore them once."

My wife is even guiltier of this than I am. Every time she opens her mouth now I hear my mother-in-law's voice coming out. I'd give you a few examples, but I fear she too is not above suing me.

28. LOVE AND HEARTACHE

After my son had been in kindergarten for a couple of weeks, he came home with big news: he was engaged to be married.

Now call me stodgy, call me old-fashioned, but I've always felt that 5 years old was just a little too young to make that kind of a commitment. After all, who was this girl? I hadn't even met her. Certainly he hadn't known her long himself.

As you can imagine, I thought this was just adorable — one of my son's many phases that would probably be forgotten about in a day or two. But shortly thereafter, I went to his classroom for a parents' event when a woman came up to me and introduced herself as my son's future mother-in-law.

These things happen so much faster than when I was a kid. But it was a phase that never seemed to go away. One day when he was in a gift shop with my wife, he insisted on buying wedding rings for himself and his fiancée. She happily obliged.

All this brought me back to my youth. When I was his age, I had the soul of a poet and fell in love with every other girl I met. The difference between me and him is that in kindergarten, I was way too shy to even talk to a girl, let alone ask for her hand in marriage.

But to the boy, these things seemed to come easy, and all was well, until one day. He was out with his mother and casually announced to her that his betrothed had dumped him. What's worse, he heard about it second hand, and he had no idea why. Girls are so confusing, he told me. I tried to comfort him by explaining that they only get worse as they get older. It didn't seem to work.

I felt terrible for him. There's nothing worse than the "pangs of disprized love" as Shakespeare put it. I thought back to rejections I had endured in my youth — how they were worse than any illness or injury I had ever suffered. I was ready to be there for him in his hour of need.

The next day he came home and told me that they were no longer broken up and had a wonderful time together on the bus ride home, laughing all the way. Indeed, there's nothing more fickle than the heart of a 6-year-old girl.

But while it's easy to dismiss the romance of a couple of little kids, I can remember myself clearly at that age. It was my first day of first grade and there was a new girl in the school. She had long brown hair, seemed just a little bit nervous, and most importantly, she laughed at my jokes. I was smitten. She was truly the embodiment of feminine perfection in my little mind. My future was clear. We'd soon be living a life of marital bliss.

Alas, it wasn't to be. A few years later, her family moved out of town and she no longer attended our school. She was out of my life forever.

I remember in the early days of social media, when my friends were trying to convince me to join Facebook, one of the carrots they dangled in front of me was the chance to get to see what old friends were doing now. Each of them regaled me with a tale of how they looked up an old crush, only to discover that the years were unkind and she had somehow turned into a hideous monster. They took delight in this, as though it made them feel vindicated somehow.

Well, eventually, my first-grade love contacted me via Facebook and I was eager to share the experience of seeing what a troll she turned into. Unfortunately, she was stunningly beautiful. It seems the universe doesn't always dole out the vindication to everybody.

The point of all this — and yes, I do have one — is that all these guys remembered these girls as though it were yesterday. Although the romance of a couple of first-graders may seem cute — or worse, meaningless — just try to think back to how you felt at the time, and remember that the emotional wounds of the playground can leave some of the deepest scars.

I'm not saying you should book a reception venue for your kindergartners; but I am saying that you shouldn't dismiss their little intrigues either. Sure, you can look at it laughingly through the wisdom of years, but to them it's a very real thing.

And when their little hearts are broken, you should be there for them — and at least hope that those who broke their hearts turn into grown-up trolls some day.

29. TRICKING YOUR CHILDREN

My son came into the world in 2007, meaning by law he was born with an inherent ability to use a computer. To folks of my parents' generation, a computer is a scary monster — a necessary evil that sits in their den just waiting for the moment when it can jump up and attack them.

But my son couldn't be more at home in front of a computer if he had a tiny little tablet in utero. For him, there's no novelty — and there's no fear. I think my parents' biggest fear with computers is that they're going to do something to break it. Since that thought never entered my son's head, he manipulates it with the deftness of a concert virtuoso.

One day, I found him on Google Earth searching through what appeared to be a blank white screen. When I asked him what he was doing, he told me he was in the polar ice caps searching for Santa's workshop. I wasn't sure how to respond to this. My first gut feeling was that I should tell him he was wasting his time. Then I thought it would be terrible to destroy the boy's illusions. After going back and forth and giving it a lot of deep parental thought, I said to him: "Oh. OK."

I knew as determined as he was, he'd still give up eventually. And you'd think I'd be wracked with guilt knowing my son was wasting his time looking for a needle that was nowhere to be found in this particular haystack.

But I didn't. That's because when you're a parent, you trick your kids all the time.

As I've mentioned before, my daughter would never eat anything but pancakes and macaroni & cheese; so when my son came along, I was determined to make sure he had a more sophisticated palate. I knew the only way to do this was to trick him.

It was simple really. What food do children want most of all? Is it candy? Is it cupcakes? Is it potato chips or french fries?

Nope. The food kids want the most is whatever it is you happen to be eating. If you ask a child to try something — even beg them — they will decide they don't like it before even sampling it. But if you tell them they can't have any, then they decide they love it. And so I used this psychological trick with my son often. And it paid off. At the ripe old age of 6, his favorite dish is roast duckling and his favorite snack is frozen peas — that's right, frozen peas, not cooked, not even thawed. He pops them like candy. So not only did I get him to eat something healthy — I don't even have to cook it for him.

So I used trickery and deceit to get him to this point, but it's incredibly refreshing to have a kid whose diet is not limited to hot dogs and chicken nuggets. In fact, he's turned into quite the culinary thrillseeker. The only problem is that he enjoys a lot of food my wife just doesn't care for. So he and I are usually on our own when we have something exotic.

Tricking your kids comes in handy at other times, too. My son, like a lot of children these days, seems to acquire a lot of stuff. With extended families and grandparents living longer, kids get quite the haul at birthdays and Christmas. Whenever these occasions near, my wife and I always panic a little bit, because we worry about where we're going to fit all the toys the boy is going to accumulate.

So we have the semi-annual toy purge. The only way he can get new toys is to get rid of some of the old ones he's outgrown. We give the toys he's no longer interested in to charity. The only problem is that he doesn't want to give up anything. So I have to do it surreptitiously.

Initially, I tried appealing to his sense of reason, and he sympathized with me, truly he did. So I lined up all his stuffed animals and asked him which he'd be willing to part with.

One by one, we went through them all, only to find that he wanted to keep each and every one of them — even though he never plays with them. So I had to come up with another plan. Here's where the trickery comes in. He had so many that I figured I could get rid of about one a week without him noticing.

Slowly but surely, I thinned out the herd. Only once or twice did he ever say anything about a missing toy. I responded by quickly changing the subject and pointing his attention in a different direction.

Another useful technique is what I call the "lesser of two evils trick." There was a time when my son would get really dramatic every time I told him to do something that he really didn't want to do. I'd diffuse the situation by giving him a choice. Only I'd let him choose between something he hated and something he really, really hated. For instance, he always hated taking a bath. Instead of telling him he had to take one, I'd ask him, "Which do you want to do, take a bath, or take a trip to the grocery store?"

Now, he hated going to the grocery store, so he'd pick the bath. He'd do it begrudgingly, but it was less traumatic for him because, after all, it was his decision. Kids love feeling they're in control, even when they're clearly not.

Just remember, this only works up to a point. Eventually, the boy learned how to call my bluff. I'd give him the same choice when he knew the last thing I wanted to do was go to the grocery store. So he'd look at me like he was looking right through me and say, "Let's go to the grocery store."

So again, I'd have to distract him — "Hey, why don't you go on Google Earth and search for Santa Claus?"

OK, sometimes I do feel a little guilty.

30. IN THE EVENT OF AN EMERGENCY

One day my son came home from kindergarten and said, "Daddy, we need to talk." So we sat down on the couch and he said, "Daddy, I need to know your emergency plan."

He didn't even need to elaborate. I knew exactly what he was talking about. The emergency plan. Boy, that really took me back. I remember the day in kindergarten when the firefighters came to visit our school. We were all herded into the gym where we were taught how to stop, drop and roll, and we were shown what a firefighter in full gear looks like, so we wouldn't be afraid of one if we saw him break into our flame-filled bedrooms in the middle of the night.

It was always exciting to leave the classroom when you were in kindergarten, but that wasn't even the best part — we actually got to go outside. There, parked right in front of the school, was a huge ladder truck. And way at the top of the ladder was a hapless, shaking volunteer who was trying to summon the courage to jump off the ladder into one of those big trampoline things the other firefighters were holding.

At the time, I thought this was the bravest man I had ever seen. Looking back, I realize it was probably the department's newest volunteer, and this was some sort of hazing ritual. After waiting for what seemed about half an hour, the terrified recruit finally threw caution to the wind and jumped. He lived to tell the tale.

I remember I too had come home all excited, demanding to know my father's emergency plan. I believe his exact words were, "If the house is on fire, leave."

When he saw that his answer was completely unsatisfactory, he went into more detail: "Leave your bedroom, go down the hall, and go out the front door."

This made sense, of course, but I was somehow hoping for something more dramatic and adventurous. I sensed that the boy was also looking for something more substantial, so I tried to show him how important it was by testing the smoke detectors so he could know what they sound like. Then I told him to come out his bedroom door if he ever heard that sound in the middle of the night, and we'd meet in the hallway.

About a week or two later, I was doing some late night cooking that set off the smoke detector. The kind of detectors I have are hard-wired to the house, so when one goes off, they all go off. It sounded like London during the Blitz. Realizing that my son, who had long since gone to bed, was probably in a full state of panic (especially since one of the blaring smoke detectors is right above his bed) I raced to his room to calm him down. I threw open his door only to discover that he hadn't even woken up. That's right, the same kid who was so adamant about having an escape route and an emergency plan was fast asleep among the house's blaring alarms. My wife peeked around my shoulder at him and said, "Well, that's not good."

So there's a new emergency plan. If we have a fire, or a nuclear war or a zombie apocalypse, the first thing I'll have to do is go and wake up my son so he can enjoy it with the rest of us.

One thing that surprised me about his emergency preparedness visit from the local fire department is that they didn't give him a window sticker. One of the most exciting things about the firefighters when I was in kindergarten was that they gave us these oval reflective stickers that said "TOT FINDER" to put in our bedroom windows.

Those things were great for providing me with an added sense of security. But they also adhered to the window with the tensile strength of steel. My sticker remained there long after I was no longer a tot.

"Daddy, I need to know your emergency plan."

In fact, when I had abandoned my parents' home to strike out on my own, it was still there, even though there were no more tots to rescue. I think the sticker remained until my parents finally bought replacement windows for their elderly home.

I wonder if these stickers still remain on the windows of my classmates in their old houses. Maybe that's why the firefighters didn't bother handing them out to my son's class. They probably got tired of taking the trouble to smash in through a window only to find a bunch of unused exercise equipment because that's what their empty-nest parents turned their kids' old rooms into.

But the whole thing got me to thinking of other emergency situations, and I wanted to make sure my son knew everything he was supposed to know in the event of an emergency.

"Do you know your address?" I asked him."

He thought for about 30 seconds before answering, "No. No, I don't."

"Well, let's start by telling me what state you live in," I said.

"America?"

Clearly, we had a lot of work to do. I asked him if he could at least tell me the number to call in an emergency.

"Oh, I know that," he answered with confidence. "It's 1-9-9."

Eventually, we got the whole thing straightened out; and I'm happy to report that he knows exactly what to do if I happen to drop dead some day — that is, if he manages to wake up.

EPILOGUE.

MY PROMISE TO MY SON

ON HIS 5TH BIRTHDAY

I do not have it in me to be a "tiger parent" or a "helicopter parent" so I will never push you toward greatness or wealth or fame.

But you will learn what it means to be noble.

You will act honorably with every man. You will respect every woman. You will be kind to every animal.

You will learn that violence is not strength and that compassion is not weakness. You will learn this before you set foot in kindergarten.

You will always remove your hat when the flag passes in a parade.

You will remember that your language is the language of Shakespeare, Milton, Keats and Tennyson. You will treat it with respect.

I will introduce you to every belief and non-belief and leave it up to your conscience which you choose to follow. But you will respect everyone's beliefs — and non-beliefs.

You will learn that it's perfectly OK to strike out.

You will never belittle anyone's accomplishments. You will never find joy in anyone's tragedies.

I will give you my advice — anytime you ask for it. But only when you ask for it.

You will know the meaning of courage and valor. You will learn this not on a battlefield or in a fistfight. You will learn it the very first time you find yourself standing up for something when everybody else is sitting down. This is the hardest thing you will ever do.

You will learn that winning and losing are unimportant, but that trying is everything. It's hard to understand, but there is no such thing as a real victory — or a real defeat.

You will come to appreciate freedom more than anything else you possess. You will allow nobody to take it away.

You will always detest every form of prejudice — racism, sexism, homophobia. You will hate these things as you hate filth.

You will look everyone directly in the eye when you speak to him. You will listen to everyone, whether it be king or crazy man. And you may just find one day that there is nothing mightier than the meek.

You will learn self-reliance, yet you will never be afraid to ask for help.

You will be afraid. Fear is an inescapable part of life. You will learn to live with fear and never let it control you.

You will endure pain. You will have cuts, scrapes, heartache, loss, maybe even a broken bone or two. As much as I may want to keep you from these things, I will never deprive you of these experiences, for I have learned they are all a part of growth. You will come to learn this as well.

You will follow your heart to wherever it takes you, even if it takes you far away from me. I will never make you feel guilty for it.

You will always remember that love is the most powerful thing in the world.

9287605R00099

Made in the USA
San Bernardino, CA
10 March 2014